Panchayats, Women and Health for All

Institute of Social Sciences

The Institute of Social Sciences was founded in 1985, to study contemporary social, political and economic issues and problems, in an inter-disciplinary perspective and to make available its findings and recommendations to government bodies, social scientists, policy makers, people's and workers' organizations, so as to widen their options for action. The evolution of an informed and action-oriented public opinion is the primary aim of the Institute.

The research projects undertaken by the Institute cover a wide range of subjects in the areas of local governance, women's studies, environment and contemporary economic and political issues. The Institute also organizes seminars, workshops, discussions and training programmes for the exchange of ideas and dissemination of its research findings.

The major research thrust of the Institute is in the areas of Local Governance (Panchayati Raj), Urban Studies and Economic Affairs.

The Institute seeks to build a community of concerned scholars and activists for ushering in a humane and just society.

Chairman
Dr. George Mathew
Director
Dr. Ash Narain Roy

About the Editor

Bidyut Mohanty, heads the Women's Studies Unit at the Institute of Social Sciences (ISS), New Delhi. She is also a Visiting Research Fellow at the Orfalea Center, Global and International Studies Program at the University of California, Santa Barbara.

As a convener of the ISS's annual all-India conference of Women Panchayat Representatives, she has played an active role in promoting women's empowerment and gender justice through strengthening women leadership at the grassroots. Her research areas are women's development, the political economy of culture and the impact of the food crisis in a historical perspective.

Her publications include:

Series Editor (1995-2012), *Women's Political Empowerment Day Celebrations* (New Delhi, ISS).

Editor (2011), *Local Governance: Search for New Path* (New Delhi, Concept.)

Editor (2013), *Women and Micro Credit in a Cross Cultural Perspective* (University of California, Santa Barbara, USA).

She has also authored several short stories in Odia. Her latest volume, *Gali Aaili Bhramanaru Kahani*, was published by Odisha Book Store in 2013.

Women's Political Empowerment Day Celebrations 2012

PANCHAYATS, WOMEN AND HEALTH FOR ALL

Edited by

Bidyut Mohanty

UN WOMEN

United Nations Entity for Gender Equality and the Empowerment of Women

ROYAL NORWEGIAN EMBASSY

Institute of Social Sciences

CONCEPT PUBLISHING COMPANY PVT. LTD.

NEW DELHI-110059

ISBN-13 : 978-93-5125-063-0

First Published 2014

Published and Printed by

Concept Since 1974

Concept Publishing Company Pvt. Ltd.
A/15-16, Commercial Block, Mohan Garden
New Delhi-110059 (India)
T: 25351460, 25351794, *F*: 091-11-25357109
E: publishing@conceptpub.com, W: www.conceptpub.com
Editorial Office: H-13, Bali Nagar, New Delhi-110 015, India.

Cataloging in Publication Data—*Courtesy:* D.K. Agencies (P) Ltd. <docinfo@dkagencies.com>

Women's Political Empowerment Day Celebrations (2012 : New Delhi, India)
Panchayats, women and health for all : Women's Political Empowerment Day Celebrations, 2012 / Bidyut Mohanty (ed.).
p. cm.
Includes bibliographical references and index.
ISBN 9789351250630

1. Women—Political activity—India—Congresses. 2. Women in development—India--Congresses. 3. Panchayat—India—Congresses. 4. Rural health services—India—Congresses. 5. National Rural Health Mission (India)—Congresses. I. Mohanty, Bidyut. II. Institute of Social Sciences (New Delhi, India) III. Title.

DDC 305.420954 23

Foreword

The Institute of Social Sciences has been organizing the annual Women's Political Empowerment Day Celebrations on April 24 since 1994. This red-letter day marks the anniversary of the 73rd Constitution Amendment that reserved not less than one-third seats for women in the three tiers of local government—the panchayats.

When women get elected to the panchayats, due to lack of community support, they face challenges in carrying out their constitutional roles with confidence. Those from marginalized sections of society face worst challenges. Our Institute, therefore, decided to bring together the women panchayat members to New Delhi for an annual event, where they could build support base by interacting with each other as well as with women political leaders, activists and experts. Over the years the Women's Political Empowerment Day celebrations have not only strengthened the women panchayat leaders' confidence and capacity to bring about social change in their villages, but also provided an opportunity to increase solidarity with women leaders from other parts of the country.

If women in our villages, and especially the elected women representatives, believe that panchayats are their future, they could be the effective change agents. Since they are part of the third tier of the government—the district, the block and the village panchayats—the elected sarpanchs are Chief Ministers of their panchayats and have a cabinet that is the council of panchs. The Assembly is the *gram sabha*, the mandatory meetings of all voters in the village. Today, the reality is that the third tier of government and its institutions are marginalized.

Local democratic governance, however, has deep roots in India. We have had republics in India even before the ones in Greece, over 2500 years ago. The *Linchvi ganatantra* in present-day Vaishali (Bihar) is an example of such institutions (see Annexure IV). Today, gram sabha is the continuation of those assemblies. But if gram sabha meetings are not held, then how can the people govern the villages? How can health, sanitation and safety in our villages work? We can achieve positive local change through participatory governance only. The democratically elected members and presidents of panchayats have the responsibility to ensure that every one, irrespective of economic status, caste or religion, has a say in local decision-making.

If the elected representatives and sarpanchs especially women do not take firm decisions and take the responsibilities according to the 73rd Constitution Amendment, then panchayats will be controlled by Members of Parliament (MPs), Members of Legislative Assemblies (MLAs), Collectors, Block Development Officers (BDOs) and Panchayat Secretaries.

Since 1994, every year this national gathering had deliberated upon a theme relevant to village life. Elected women representatives interact with subject experts, women leaders, and present their own experiences. In the process, they gain confidence to face difficulties with the support of their peers. The theme for 2012 was "Panchayats, Women and Health for All".

Given our country's dismal human development indicators in areas such as high incidence of malnourishment, infant mortality and maternal mortality, we wanted to find out the extent to which women representatives in panchayats were aware of the government's various health-related programmes and how they were associated with such initiatives. Therefore, during the national conference we conducted a survey. The survey showed quite clearly that even though members of panchayats in general and women in particular have the right to look after the health plans and monitor the local healthcare services, many health schemes are developed without consulting women panchayat members and implemented exclusively by government departments. If women in local government do not have a voice in local health programmes, who will listen to ordinary women in the village?

Without women's full participation in governance, there is no democracy. The reservation of 50 per cent of the seats for women in panchayats implemented by 14 states, is a milestone in India's democratic development. Making use of all available instruments, let us now aim to create a great nation—India.

I hope this publication will open the eyes of the decision makers and entice them to make policies from below which will empower common villagers through the local government system. I acknowledge the financial support of UN Women and the Royal Norwegian Embassy for making the 2012 Women's Political Empowerment Day Celebrations a great success.

George Mathew
Chairman
Institute of Social Sciences

Acknowledgements

The volume, 'Panchayats, Women and Health for All' is the result of a team work including numerous elected women representatives from all over the country and the panel of speakers. We are grateful to them for their inputs. We are also thankful to Ms. Jehanara Wasi who meticulously edited the volume. Thanks are also due to the Institute's computer person Mr. Nanda Kumar who worked hard to give the final touches to the layout. Finally, we are profusely thankful to the UN Women and the Norwegian Embassy for their financial support without which this volume would not have seen the light of the day.

Bidyut Mohanty
Head, Women's Studies
Institute of Social Sciences

Contents

1
Introduction

Bidyut Mohanty

Over 550 elected women representatives from 20 states participated in the 19th Women's Political Empowerment Day Celebrations. At least two-thirds of the elected women representatives (EWRs) were ward members of the gram panchayats, followed by sarpanchs, block level panchayat members, zilla panchayat members and a few *parshads* from Chhattisgarh. Besides, members of Self-Help Groups (SHGs) panchayat secretaries, DRDA personnel, motivators and members of civil societies also attended the three-day programme. This time, five state governments such as Arunachal Pradesh, Assam, Goa, Tamil Nadu and Sikkim sponsored elected women representatives to the national event.

This year's theme 'Panchayats, Women and Health for All' is important for the women in general, and panchayats in particular, as panchayats have been assigned the 29 subjects of which health including sanitation, safe drinking water, shelter, etc., occupies an important place. Secondly, the Government of India has declared the Twelfth Five Year Plan as the plan for health to achieve inclusive growth by reaching out to the excluded communities with equitable as well as affordable healthcare facilities by availing cashless treatment. In other words, right to health has become the motto recently.

In addition, this year marks the end of the National Rural Health Mission (NRHM) which was launched in 2005. In this

Flagship scheme the panchayats have an important role in planning and implementing as well as monitoring the health-related schemes as well as to be the convergence point of health-related departments. Besides, women are always in charge of the health-related issues both in private and public spheres. Finally, India is trying to achieve the Millennium Development Goals by 2015 by reducing maternal mortality, infant mortality, and the burden of many other new and old diseases by improving health conditions.

Opening Session

The opening session of the three-day Women's Political Empowerment Day Programme began with great fanfare on April 24 at Vishwa Yuvak Kendra, New Delhi. The welcome song by the Gavaniar group from Bikaner, Rajasthan enthralled all. The gist of my welcome address is the following.

April 24 is an auspicious day for various reasons. First of all it is celebrated as Women's Political Empowerment Day. Secondly, this year it coincided with Akshya Tritiya Day, which is socially very important all over India. Finally, the government is observing April 24 as panchayat day.

April 24 is observed as Women's Political Empowerment Day as it was on this day in 1993, the 73rd Constitutional Amendment became a part of the Constitution of India and brought a new lease of life to the panchayats. This historic amendment made provisions to reserve not less than one-third of the total seats for women in the three-tier Panchayati Raj System. It became necessary because our society is a patriarchal society and in this society women do not play any role in the decision-making body. In order to fill the void, the policy makers made the provision of reserving at least one-third of the seats in the panchayats which has been raised to fifty per cent recently by several states.

Women who come to the panchayats through reservation are mostly first timers and they contest the election prodded by family members. In order to build their confidence and cement the solidarity as also to create an awareness about their role in politics, the Institute decided to observe April 24 as the Women's Political Empowerment Day. It was first started in 1994.

Rita Sarin, Country Representative, the Hunger Project, India chaired the first session. In her enthusiastic way, she observed that since the first day of the reservation, women started working efficiently. She also recommended that health-related issues should be transferred to EWRs only.

Shradha Chauhan, sarpanch, Kheda Panchayat, Alwar District, shared her views on health, sanitation and environment. Following in Gandhiji's footsteps, she equated health with happiness. According to her, one gets happiness, only if one has control over his/her body and mind. She also talked about cleanliness in order to have a congenial environment. The habit of cleanliness starts from one's own home, she said emphatically. One should not only keep one's own house clean but also try to keep the environment clean. She traced the causal link between open defecation and incidence of diarrhoea. She cautioned the women in panchayats to be aware of that causal link and start creating awareness among the villagers.

In his welcome address, Suraj Kumar, Head, Governance Programme, UN WOMEN referred to two pledges—one to achieve universal primary healthcare and the other—women's representation in panchayats. The first one was a worldwide pledge which is known as the Alma Ata Declaration or health for all. It was signed in 1978 in Kazakstan. It was pledged to achieve health for all within a span of ten years. The second one was made in 1993 to strengthen the panchayats, and to enhance the women's participation in local government more effectively that was India-specific. On both fronts considerable progress has been made, he reported. On the first pledge, there has been a reduction in the infant mortality rate. On the second front, the panchayats have become an integral part of our political system. Women's participation in panchayats is becoming increasingly visible. To date if somebody tries to dismiss the statement that women in panchayats are not aware of the health issues nobody would take it seriously.

However, there is still a mismatch between the thought and action. Suraj Kumar referred to an incident in which the Digvijay Singh government in Madhya Pradesh, tried to hand over the control of the health department to panchayats and immediately the doctors struck saying that the panchayat members had no ideas regarding the health issue! Finally he requested the women to suggest practical solutions to health problems.

K.B. Saxena, Council for Social Development, New Delhi, said that no other country has taken up such a step as to bring women on a large scale from the societal fold to the political fold by the stroke of a pen. It is revolutionary because women have taken charge of developmental work of the village in addition to household work. Today, women are struggling to get seats in the Assembly and the Parliament. Women's presence in the panchayats, has instilled self-confidence among them. Earlier government officers did not care for the village women and women could raise their agenda only through the men of the household. But nowadays the officers approach women to consult them and if they visit the officers, they are offered seats. He further added, health is the foundation of development and health problems are continuously complex. There are many government schemes regarding health but those schemes are not implemented properly. As the leaders of panchayats, it is the duty of women to know about those schemes and try to implement them properly so that everybody in the village will benefit. He also mentioned that all the health-related departments are working sectorally, that this must be coordinated by the panchayats. Renu Wadhera, senior advisor, Royal Norwegian Embassy observed that whenever she meets an elected woman representative, she acquires energy and strength. She wondered whether the elected women representatives took up health issues at all, especially at the Gram Sabha. In this interactive session there were several responses. For instance, a Pradhan from West Bengal stated: even though issues such as functioning of Integrated Child Development Services (ICDS), sanitation and other health-related issues should be raised in the Gram Sabha by women, in some states she visited, women don't attend the meetings. At the same time, she added that the case of West Bengal is different. In West Bengal not only do women attend the Gram Sansad, but they also discuss development issues including health.

Diverse System of Treatment: Implications for the Panchayats

Kamal Nayan Kabra, Malcolm Adeseshiah Chair Professor, ISS chaired the session: Madhulika Banerjee, Department of Political Science, Delhi University and Natasha Das, the freelance cancer specialist, shared their views on the alternative system of treatment. Madhulika Banerjee pointed out that each culture has its own traditional system of treatment for the indigenously prevalent diseases. Those systems of knowledge should be revived and standardized. She also talked about a Foundation which has been set up in Bangalore to revitalize Natu Vaidya's (people's) knowledge. With an effort to revitalize the traditional knowledge, the government has also started a branch of the traditional system of treatment called Ayush under the National Rural Health Mission (NRHM). Further, the Twelfth Five Year Plan has been described as the Plan of Health. The women in panchayats have an important role to play in NRHM. She hoped that the women present here would seize the opportunity and would try to revive the great tradition of people's knowledge on health. Natasha Das, during her speech, gave some important tips on how to save oneself from various types of women-specific cancers. It is important because women are the first ones to look after the health of the family but the last ones to attend to their own health.

In the second part of the session, two doctors from Los Angeles (USA), gave demonstrations about the easily accessible small health kits to diagnose the nature of common diseases such as blood pressure, diabetes, etc. It is interesting to note that both the doctors were flooded with many queries particularly relating to availability of the small kits. After the interactive sessions and plenary an evening of cultural programmes followed that was organized by Wisdom Arts and Cultural Academy. They presented a unique blend of traditional and modern dance. It was a memorable experience for the women representatives.

Inaugural Session and Award Giving Ceremony

George Mathew, Chairman, ISS in his welcome address, highlighted the developments since the 73rd Constitutional Amendment. According to him, millions of women in India are entering public life and wherever they now have freedom and power, remarkable changes are taking place.

Award Giving Ceremony

Four outstanding panchayat women leaders— Shashi Kiran, Member of Zilla Parishad, Lahaul and Spiti, Himachal Pradesh; Puniben C. Rajpapra, Sarpanch, Gujarat; Manisha Gadve, Sarpanch, Maharashtra; and Parbati Patra, Sarpanch, West Bengal were awarded for their excellent work. The award giving ceremony was preceded by the screening of a documentary on the life history of the previous awardees.

Greetings

Mr. Aslak Brun, Minister, Deputy Chief of Mission (DCM), Royal Norwegian Embassy, addressing the gathering at the inaugural session complimented India, the largest democracy, for its effort to deepen its democracy by reserving seats for women in the local government which resulted in women taking an active part in economic, political and legal spheres on an equal footing. He informed the audience that the Government of Norway and UN Women are helping the Government of India to strengthen the health system under NRHM so that India can achieve the Millennium Development Goals.

Fredrika Meijer, Representative, UNFPA was happy about the theme as the health of the nation depends on the women's empowerment. She observed that the introduction of the National Rural Health Mission (NRHM) is really innovative, since it has introduced a real bottom up approach to health matters by stressing the importance of village health, sanitation and nutrition committees. She exhorted the delegates to take more interest in making the health and sanitation committee effective in the coming years.

She also informed the audience that her organization is trying to convince women to space the birth of children in order to produce healthy children. It can be done by the use of contraceptive methods. The Accredited Social Health Activist (ASHA) has taken up the responsibility of spreading the above message. She also highlighted the question of female foeticide and role of a sarpanch. She pointed out that if the sarpanch takes keen interest in the issue, she could make a difference in eliminating the practice of female foeticide. She congratulated Shashi Kiran, who tried very hard to give maternity benefits to women workers even in the unorganized sector.

Finally Anne Stenhammer, Regional Programme Coordinator, UN Women, in her address pointed out that the concept of empowerment must reach every woman of the country. An elected woman must ensure that the girl child's right is honoured by sending her to school, and a little money is saved to look after the health and a small road can be built to take the surplus harvest to the nearest market. All this developmental work can be done if women get elected. Of course, we need the ballot box and casting of votes to elect the women. But we also need the support of men and boys to achieve the women's political empowerment, she reiterated. Ms. Stenhammer praised the Government of India for the quota system and requested the Panchayati Raj Ministry to really devolve funds, functions and functionaries so that the decentralized decision-making process starts in the true sense of the term. It is so because people live in the villages and the decision should be taken at the grass roots level. She also requested the elected women representatives (EWRs) saying that they should encourage other women to take part in politics so that just like them, the other women can also take decisions in certain matters and work towards the gender equality.

Inaugural Address

Honourable Union Minister for Panchayati Raj and Tribal Affairs, V. Kishore Chandra Deo delivered the inaugural address. He acknowledged the central role of women in the areas of health, particularly that of panchayats. He said that at present one-third of total seats in panchayats have been reserved for women and many states including Andhra Pradesh have raised the quota to fifty per cent. Referring to the quota system he noted that by increasing the sheer number of seats may not bring real empowerment to women. He also drew attention to two conflicting trends—while in some states women are really guided by their male family members but in others women don't listen to men any longer. He said one was to deal with both situations and added that April 24 is being celebrated as Panchayat Diwas by the Government of India to encourage the states to make panchayats more effective. In order to encourage states to devolve more powers, the state governments are being awarded on that day. He pointed out that in 2011, Haryana got an award for having the best panchayati raj system even though it is an established fact that panchayats are working well in Kerala, Karnataka, and West Bengal. The Chief Minister, Bhupender Singh himself received the award. That created great enthusiasm among the people. He also talked about the inter-linkage between health, role of women in panchayats and sanitation. Talking about Nirmal Puraskar, he said that so far about 28,000 panchayats have been given awards for achieving total sanitation. He also exhorted women to work towards the nirmal gram.

Keynote Address

Vandana Prashad, Founding Secretary and National Convener of Public Health Resource Network chaired the session. She highlighted the importance of mental health by saying that depression and anxiety are common features of women's health complaints. The current programme for mental health is very weak with poor integration within NRHM.

Ritu Priya, Professor, Centre for Social Medicine and Community Health, Jawaharlal Nehru University, New Delhi, delivered the keynote address. While addressing the audience, Ritu Priya said that there are two liberative ideas prevalent in the history of mankind. The first one is women's empowerment and the other one is health for all. On both fronts some results have been achieved but in the present globalized world, the achievements have been blunted. At present however, schemes like NRHM have provided some opportunities for the panchayats in general and women in panchayats in particular in the form of reintroducing Ayush, creating the cadre of ASHA, encouraging the formation of village sanitation and health committees, etc. Women can seize the opportunities and try to make it functional. At the same time she highlighted the fact that the primary health centres are served only by the Ayush doctors and it may lead to many health issues unaddressed. Further, she requested each panchayat to take an oath today that nobody should sleep hungry and no sick person should be isolated or left alone without proper treatment.

Plenary

Can one maintain good health where there are no doctors? That was a critical issue discussed in the plenary session. Saurabh Gehlot, Medical Superintendent Vinayak Hospital, Noida was positive on this question, if the community adopts preventive measures including traditional methods. Nupur Tiwari, Assistant Professor, Indian Institute of Public Administration (IIPA), New Delhi chaired the session and shed light on the indicators of women's health.

Valedictory Session

Varsha Das, former Director, National Gandhi Museum, addressed the valedictory session. She emphasized the fact that health should be treated in a holistic way in which both mental and physical health are included. In order to substantiate her point, she quoted Mahatma Gandhi. In his book *The Health Guide,* he wrote that, "Only that man (woman) can be said to be really healthy who has a sound mind in a sound body. The relation between the body and the mind is so intimate that if either of them goes out of order the whole system would suffer". Earlier, George Mathew, Chairperson, ISS introduced Varsha Das, and addressed the EWRs. He requested the EWRs to convene the Gram Sabha regularly, because it is the assembly of the third-tier government system and they are the chief ministers of their panchayats. In order to get clean drinking water, health, etc., the EWRs should convene the Gram Sabha regularly and discuss those issues. If the EWRs take up their responsibilities seriously and function effectively, then the concept of participatory democracy will be truly meaningful, he advised.

Voices from the Field

Women delegates were divided into three groups. One group discussed 'NRHM and Sex Selective Abortions'. This group was chaired by Bijayalaksmi Nanda, Miranda House, Delhi University (DU). Tulsi Patel, Department of Sociology, DU chaired the second group which discussed 'Government Health Policy and Women: Implications for the Life Cycle Problems'. Suparna Ganguly, State Institute of Rural Development (SIRD), Kalyani, West Bengal, chaired the third group which addressed the issues relating to 'Health Insurance and Women'. The views of the delegates were presented by S. Shyamala, Ghanshyam Khuswaha and Suparna Ganguly in the plenary session which was chaired by Almas Ali, senior fellow, ISS.

Asha Devi Sharma Jaipur, Rajasthan talked about registering the ultra sound machines at the panchayat level. She also suggested that the panchayats should take charge of keeping the records of deaths and births. Sarita Singh, sarpanch, Ghazipur, revealed that no standing committee has been formed in her panchayat nor has any fund come to that committee though six standing committees including Rogi Kalyan Samiti exist on paper. She also said ASHA accepts money to help pregnant women. Krishna, a ward member, Kharia Mirza Panchayat, Bhopal said that her panchayat has adopted a slogan, '*beti hai to kal hai*'. Sharada Devi, zilla panchayat member, Gorakhpur pointed out that girls are killed because poor families are unable to pay dowry and hence they resort to sex selection abortions. In order to ensure some income for women, she has organized a group of women who go and fight with the pradhan to get employment under MGNREGA so that they do not feel helpless.

K. Lal Muni, ward member Bojhwa panchayat, Ghazipur, was quite enthusiastic about the strength of her group. She in her own dialect told the audience that to begin with the male sarpanch did not share any information with them. So in order to counter that she along with her friend organized about 100 to 200 women. Those women in turn started meeting separately and discussed issues like quality and quantity of foodgrains available in PDS, access to safe drinking water in anganwadi centres, non-availability of medicines in PHC, sanitation, etc. and later insisted that the Gram Sabha should consider those issues. She also pointed out that her panchayat has started a campaign against the 'kanya bhrunohatya' or female foeticide. The women's group is also preparing a skit on the value of the girl child. Tija Devi, ward member Lachmipur, Gorakhpur, has been elected for the fourth time to her panchayat. She worked on the financial inclusion of women from the marginalized group by opening an account in the bank in their name. She talked about the activities of ASHA as to how she has been tracking down the pregnant women and takes them to the hospital.She also propagates the use of organic manure. In addition, she has campaigned against liquor.

2

Celebrating Women's Political Empowerment Day*

George Mathew

It gives me great pleasure in welcoming you all to this year's Women's Political Empowerment Day Celebrations. This is the nineteenth year of the celebrations.

As you all know, April 24, 1993 was a historic day. That was the day which set in motion a silent revolution in Indian society—minimum one-third of the seats in the local government institutions reserved for women. Now, we have more than 30 lakh men and women getting elected to the local bodies every five years. And more than one-third of them are women. When this revolutionary step was taken in this country, there was considerable apprehension, whether this would work. With our traditions, our culture and patriarchal society will there be even enough candidates to contest the seats reserved for them? But all the critics and pessimists were silenced. Another issue was will women face problems when they enter public life? In fact, they have been facing problems. Many women had to fight against severe odds on a day-to-day basis and sacrifice their lives. But today the positive side is that they are assuring the country a new era of gender equality.

---

* This was the Welcome Address delivered by Dr. George Mathew, Chairman, Institute of Social Sciences, New Delhi.

When the 73rd Constitutional Amendment became part of the Constitution on 24th April, the Institute of Social Sciences decided that this red-letter day must be observed as 'Women's Political Empowerment Day' every year. I am happy that with the support of many organizations, national and international, we could celebrate this day in the last 19 years successfully and now it has become a national event.

Elected women representatives on the whole are doing commendable work in the panchayats. I am very happy that today, we have with us panchayat women representatives from 20 states. It is an important occasion because women have come together to show their solidarity.

This year's theme is "Panchayats, Women and Health for All". The subject is timely as well as critical in the present-day situation confronting our country.

I specially thank the Hon'ble Union Minister for Panchayati Raj Shri V. Kishore Chandra Deo for accepting our invitation to be the chief guest of this programme. Deoji is very dear to the women and men who are elected as members of panchayats. He is a lover of panchayats and his work to strengthen panchayats is well recognized.

My special thank to Ms. Anne F. Stenhammer, Regional Programme Director, UNIFEM, for sponsoring this YEAR'S WOMEN'S Political Empowerment Day programme. UN Women's support to our programmes needs mention here. It is also very important that Mr. Aslak Brun, Minister-Counsellor/Deputy Chief of Mission, Royal Norwegian Embassy in New Delhi; and Mrs. Frederika Meijer, Representative, UNFPA, New Delhi and friends and well-wishers of this programme and seriously concerned with the issues of panchayati raj system in the country are guests of honour today.

Friends, let us a give our chief guests a warm welcome.

In 1999, the Institute of Social Sciences instituted the Best Outstanding Women Panchayat Leader Awards to recognise those women who are doing excellent work in their panchayats, whether it is village or block or district level. This year we have selected four outstanding women representatives from Himachal Pradesh, Gujarat, Maharashtra and West Bengal. Awards will be presented to them during the inaugural session.

3

Women in Panchayats to fulfil the Millennium Development Goals*

An Opportunity

Aslak Brun

Dear Sisters, I wish you a hearty welcome. You know that India is the world's largest democracy and the measures that the country has taken to ensure women's participation in the local democratic process is a source of inspiration. The key issue here is the right of an opportunity to you to participate in local and national elections on an equal footing and showing your legal, economic and social independence. With an active minister present here today we are very confident that a large number of women will be entering the position of power. My government has been collaborating with the ISS and UNWomen to celebrate Women's Empowerment Day on 24th April. My country is very positive in signing a memorandum of understanding (MoU) with the Ministry of Panchayati Raj on mutual cooperation for the local government. I also had the privilege to visit Andhra Pradesh to see the work of the local government. The year's theme is panchayats, women and health for all. On this issue, major initiatives have been taken jointly by the Indian government and that of Norway to establish and strengthen, UN

* Aslak Brun greeted the audience at the celebrations.

Millennium Goal 4 , that is to reduce child mortality and Goal 5 that is to reduce maternal mortality. I am also aware that the National Rural Health Mission is being run by the Government of India. The Mission's objective is to provide healthcare services at an affordable cost to the people, specially those who live in rural areas, particularly poor women and children. I thank the organizers for organizing this event and you who have assembled here from other places.

4
A Woman Sarpanch can Prevent Female Foeticide*

Fredrika Meijer

Dear Sisters I feel honoured to be with you. I am of the opinion that the health of the nation depends on your empowerment. Today's subject is women and health for all in India. I congratulate the Government of India for implementing the programme entitled the National Rural Health Mission (NRHM) which has a bottom-up approach. The NRHM gives great emphasis to the health and sanitation committee. I urge you to ensure a functioning health and sanitation committee in the villages. I strongly feel that the functioning of the health and sanitation committee not only depends on you but also with the support of your brothers. Similarly, if you have access to contraceptives, you can leave space between children. My organization namely, United Nations Population Fund believes that if you are able to take contraceptive pills then you can have healthy children. Our motto is crucial for a woman to have access to contraceptives, so that she can leave space between children and then has a healthier child. I am glad that all the relevant health issues related to you will be addressed at the forum. I know about the role of the ASHA worker, who provides contraceptives, napkins and all the essentials for your health. I am greatly concerned at the

* The country Representative, UNFPA, New Delhi greeted the participants.

increasing trend of female foeticide and I think that if you as a sarpanch understand the value of a girl child, you can make a great difference in rural areas to save the girl child. Finally, I congratulate Shashi Kiran, sarpanch from Himachal Pradesh, for her work and demand for extending maternity leave for one year. I hope to see you the following year again.

5

Women in Panchayats are no longer Proxy Women*

V. Kishore Chandra Deo

I am happy to be here on this occasion and yesterday, i.e., April 24, 2012, the government celebrated it as the Panchayati Raj Diwas. In my opinion the subject 'Panchayat, Women and Health for All' is very relevant in the present-day context. We are aware that health is very important for all of us and most of us know that you play a major role as far as health issues are concerned, particularly in panchayats, your respective families and surroundings in rural areas. In rural areas panchayats have a major role to play. But how we connect these three such as, health, women, and panchayats is a problem. You have to ensure that they play a major role as far as health issues are concerned. And it has to be done through the panchayats.

As far as reservation is concerned, though it is technically not less than 33 per cent, many states have given 50 per cent seats to women including Andhra Pradesh. (I come from Srikakulam, Andhra Pradesh). I have already got a proposal from the Cabinet to bring a Constitutional Amendment to raise reservations for women upto 50 per cent. It will soon become a reality. He mentioned that

* The Hon'ble Union Minister addressed the Participants at the inaugural session.

reservation for you alone is not going to solve the problem. I knew of many reports from some states show that some elected women are mostly controlled by their husbands, brothers, parents, and in-laws. At the same time from many other parts of the country, I also got reports where people have come and told me that elected women representatives do not listen to them any more. We have both sides of the story in India. But ultimately you will have to be made aware of your rights. When we talk of awareness, women's awareness is important. It is generally believed that education brings awareness. There are examples that in certain areas where women are educated and the literacy rate is high they have still not been empowered in the literal sense of the term and in many other parts of the country where there is economic backwardness, the literacy rate is low but women have gained more independence. I am proud to say that in most of our tribal societies being the North-East Areas in 6th Scheduled Areas, being in the 5th Scheduled Areas, the women among the tribal societies the kind of respect they can command, the power they have achieved is something remarkable. What we need to do is to give stress to those areas where women need awareness, where they are already aware, they need to be empowered. It is a blend or mix of the central issue which can give women a proper place in society. As long as they play the role they deserve respect.

You will be happy to know that this year for the first time we gave awards to individual panchayats. Earlier, it used to be given to states for the best practices of panchayats. It gives a sense of encouragement, a sense of participation, a sense of pride among the people who belong to that panchayat. For example, states in our country which have gone forward with panchayati raj are Kerala, Karnataka, Gujarat, Maharashtra, West Bengal but the neighbouring state Haryana was nowhere within reach. Last time when this award ceremony took place and the award was given to the State of Haryana, the Chief Minister himself came to receive the award. So during the last one year people over there showed great enthusiasm. Overall the State of Haryana has not come up to the level of the progressive states, but during the last one year what Haryana has achieved is much more than what these states put together have achieved. I would be very happy if the reservation goes beyond fifty per cent reservation, because we have the happy experience of successful women leaders heading panchayats or zilla parishads, particularly in the south which is very encouraging. I strongly feel that empowerment of women is real in intrinsic terms. As far as India is concerned, we have gone forward but need to progress further. This is something for which the cooperation of all of you is needed. One of the most important aspects of women's empowerment is the issue relating to health and sanitation. It is amazing that 28,000 panchayats have been declared free from pollution as far as sanitary problems are concerned. This is an important aspect as far as your role is concerned. But there are 2.7 lakh panchayats all over India. Of that number only 28,000 panchayats have got the Nirmal Puraskar. So one has to go a long way, he added.

6

Engendering the Panchayats to Achieve the MDGs*

Anne Stenhammer

Hon'ble Minister for Panchayati Raj and Tribal Affairs, Mr. V. Kishore Chandra Deo; Mr. Aslak Brun, Minister Counsellor, Royal Norwegian Embassy for India; Ms Bidyut Mohanty, Dr. Mathew, my colleague Fredrika, dear friends, distinguished guests, and fellow women! A very warm welcome to all of you. I am happy to be amongst you to celebrate this special day the award winners/ political empowerment day.

I want to take this opportunity to congratulate ISS for their excellent work on empowering grassroots women. The list of events and celebrations that ISS has organized for the past nineteen years is very impressive and I am happy that UN Women has been a part of this and other events organized by ISS.

The Secretary-General's Milllennium Development Goals Report 2010, reiterated that the Millennium Development Goals (MDGs) represent human needs and basic rights that every individual around the world should be able to enjoy—freedom from extreme poverty and hunger; quality education, productive and decent employment, good health and shelter; the right of girls to

* Greetings by Anne Stenhammer

be born and for women to give birth without risking their lives; and a world where environmental sustainability is a priority, and women and men live in equality. (Annexure-I).

As a UN representative, I would like to reiterate what has been stated before: "Gender equality and the empowerment of women are at the heart of the Millennium Development Goals and are preconditions for overcoming poverty, hunger and disease".

A healthy life is a key to ensuring that women are able to fight for their rights. Through our UN Women programme immunization and health issues are already being taken up in the gram sabhas including institutional delivery in hospitals. Gram Sabhas are being sensitized on their rights and entitlements from the National Rural Health Mission. So, in the words of UN Women's Under Secretary General, Michelle Bachelet, we have to make Gender Equality a "lived reality"!

In India it is estimated that we have over a million women in the panchayats. This is great news! In a country where men have traditionally had and continue to have greater authority in society, it is an achievement for women to struggle against age-old social barriers, and their own inhibitions to take up leadership roles in decision-making bodies. The Women's Empowerment Day Celebration is thus a tribute to all brave women who have decided to end inequalities and fight for their rights. I congratulate all of you who have come from across India on your struggle to end gender inequality.

I would also like to let you know that you are not alone. At UN Women, we believe that 'women's leadership is vital to a just and equitable world.

Many of you have been attending this event over the years. You have heard, and participated in the discussions on various issues related to women's empowerment. I addressed the gathering for the last two years. Today I want to ask you, how have your lives changed? What have you done for your community since the last meeting you attended? How has it been helpful to attend these meetings? Did you know that the challenges—big and small—that you face every day—from fetching water, to access to clean toilets, to travelling by road, to access to health services—are all matters that can be solved by the local government?

An effective and responsive government is one that addresses all issues of all members of its constituency including you. But a government will be responsive only when citizens like you are aware of your rights and entitlements.

There are many women in India, especially rural India, who have not been as lucky as us—who have not had the opportunity to set foot outside their own village; who have not been fortunate to experience and learn about their rights and entitlements—of how they can transform their own lives and the lives of other women. We must reach out to these women.

I would like to take this opportunity to inform you about UN Women's programme on 'Promoting Women's Political Leadership and Governance in India and South Asia'. South Asia, with a population of over 2 billion, has over 1.5 million villages with an estimated 3 million elected representatives.

In India, this programme is in collaboration with the Ministry of Panchayati Raj, Government of India. It is being implemented in Andhra Pradesh, Karnataka, Madhya Pradesh, Odisha, and Rajasthan at this initial stage. We will be working in 16 districts in these 5 states.

The programme covers over half a million elected women representatives and will improve grassroots democracy in these states for an estimated 365 million people in India. The GoI-UN Women programme is very different from other programmes of capacity building of local governance in a significant way—it focuses explicitly on the role and potential of panchayats to promote gender equality.

In this programme, it is not that women are trained to deliver for panchayats—for better village planning and project implementation. The roles are reversed—the panchayat is instead expected to deliver for women—focusing on issues that are central to the lives of India's women—physical security, political empowerment, good health, and economic security and rights.The plans of panchayats—and budgets for them—must relate directly to improving the quality of life of women, their households and communities.

The programme is also coordinating well with efforts of other UN agencies. We have signed an MoU with UNDP and UNICEF to have a common approach and work in specific states to cover more. So with not much extra money the programme can reach out to more people with a total coverage of 13 states between the three agencies.

I would like to say that this is not only about the UN and its projects. This is for you, who have come from all over India to take it forward and make it a success. For this we need change in the mindset at micro level community and locality, change in the institutions and change at macro level—national policy and global forums for a greater voice for women in gram sabhas and gram panchayats.

The Ministry of Panchayati Raj is looking at this programme as an innovative pilot. The experiences and lessons from this programme will assist the Ministry to scale it up to the entire country.

This is essential for the successful implementation of the national commitment for women's human rights and gender equality.

Just as you, I want to see more and more women in India becoming strong representatives in leadership roles; with enhanced capabilities of women leaders—both individual and collective; so that they can be assertive individuals, raise their collective voice against gender inequalities, and question social and political ideologies.

Let us join hands together to make the future of women better, just and equitable. A future where women can live free of violence, discrimination, ignorance, and poverty. Thank you.

INSTITUTE OF SOCIAL SCIENCES

Outstanding Women Panchayat Leaders Award

2012

Presented to

PUNIBEN RAJPARA

on the occasion of

Women's Political Empowerment Day Celebrations

April 25, 2012, New Delhi

Herself a BPL card holder, **Ms Puniben Rajpara,** Sarpanch of Makassar Gram Panchayat in Surendranagar District, Gujarat, has made housing facilities available for more than 40 people and other facilities under various schemes, but continues to live in a low-ceiling house where she has to bend to enter. For the last 15 years, Puniben has served the panchayat either as panchayat member or Deputy Sarpanch, and currently as the village Sarpanch. Interestingly, she won the last election from a general seat defeating two male contenders.

Water shortage was a perennial problem in her panchayat. Ms. Puniben approached the water supply department on her own and worked hard to make water facilities available to the people of the village, while her adversaries tried to get her suspended from the post of Deputy Sarpanch. Not only did she undertake construction work but also made all efforts to ensure regular employment for people in the village.

Being a member of the Water Committee formed by AKRSP helped her to make water available to everyone in the village. Besides water tanks, she also made the RCC road and water boring in the village, thus making available basic amenities to the village people. To ensure that the rooms of the school built under Sarva Shiksha Abhiyan are made properly and their construction is of acceptable quality, she is constantly present on the site neglecting her own household work.

Ms. Puniben has also been successful in motivating women to attend panchayat meetings. She strongly objected to husbands of panchayat committee members attending the meetings. Her strategy worked and the women members began to attend panchayat meetings regularly. Not only this, they also attended the gram sabha with more regularity. Most decisions concerning the development of the village are now taken in the gram sabha.

Asked why she did not avail herself of the facilities due to her as BPL holder, her reply is befitting of a model panchayat leader: "I am first the Sarpanch, then a BPL beneficiary. So I must give preference to the villagers before doing anything for myself".

This award is given to Ms. Puniben Rajpara for her outstanding work and exceptional leadership qualities.

ASH NARAIN ROY

Director

INSTITUTE OF SOCIAL SCIENCES

Outstanding Women Panchayat Leaders Award

2012

Presented to

MANISHA GADVE

on the occasion of

Women's Political Empowerment Day Celebrations

April 25, 2012, New Delhi

Ms. Manisha Gadve, Sarpanch of Kodoli Panchayat (Devgarh Block) in Kolhapur district of Maharashtra, is an outstanding example of genuine women's political empowerment. Kodoli village, 30 kms from Kolhapur city, is perhaps the first in Maharashtra to formally adopt a resolution not to discriminate against HIV/AIDS patients in the village. Inhabited by 45,000 villagers, there are 49 people, including a child, who are either HIV positive or suffering from AIDS. Kolhapur district ranks fifth in the state among high-risk areas after Mumbai, Pune, Sangli and Solapur.

Manisha Gadve got elected in 2010. Earlier she was a member of the Mahila Mandal. Given the seriousness of the issue, she involved NGOs, AIDS Control Unit members and students and began to motivate women for taking a collective pledge that they would not discriminate against anyone who was found to be HIV positive. Gadve took the lead in convincing the people how women were more vulnerable to HIV as they could transmit it to an unborn child as well. This movement began as a forum in September 2010. Today it has grown into an active, pulsating force.

Street plays were staged in the neighbouring village where an anganwadi worker had been thrown out of her job and ostracized after it was discovered that she was HIV-positive. It was at this stage women rallied behind Manisha. Ignoring HIV prejudices they responded to Manisha's call for cooperation. Thanks mainly to the support of women voters, she was able to overcome cultural hurdles as well as prejudices and could fight against discrimination against HIV/AIDS. On Republic Day, the Gram Sabha of Kodoli village adopted a special resolution directing all villagers not to discriminate against the AIDS victims.

Gadve understood that women are the best agents to understand the problems and they are the most powerful agents of change. Thus Gadve has used her leadership skills to make Kodoli a model village where HIV is neither a matter or fear, nor shame, but a manageable and preventable problem like any other.

This award is given to Ms Manisha Gadve for her imaginative leadership.

ASH NARAIN ROY

Director

INSTITUTE OF SOCIAL SCIENCES

Outstanding Women Panchayat Leaders Award

2012

Presented to

PARBATI PATRA

on the occasion of

Women's Political Empowerment Day Celebrations

April 25, 2012, New Delhi

Ms. Parbati Patra, Pradhan of Jaynagar Gram Panchayat of Purba Medinipur District of West Bengal, hails from a poor Scheduled Caste family. Patra became a member of her Gram Panchayat for the first time in 1998. She was again elected from a seat that was reserved for Scheduled Castes but not for women. Under her dynamic leadership, Jaynangar Gram Panchayat has become a model of what a gram panchayat can achieve. Meetings of Gram Panchayats including that of Gram Sansad are held regularly.

Ms. Patra has given special attention to development of women. All girl children are enrolled in school. Continuous campaigns are carried out against female foeticide and no such incident has occurred in her gram panchayat. The gram panchayat has also accomplished hundred per cent coverage under Janani Suraksha Yojana. Women are involved in the bottom-up planning process and in the gram sansad meetings. She has also carried out 116 projects under MGNREGA at a total cost of more than Rs 93 lakhs. As many as 47 families have got 100 days of work under the scheme and the average for the gram panchayat is 45 days. She has also taken a special initiative to get 18 widows remarried with financial support from the gram panchayat.

Shrimati Patra has given due attention to overall development of her gram panchayat. Three all-weather roads have been built and all the inhabitants of the Gram Panchayat got piped water. Not a single case of infant mortality or maternal mortality took place in her gram panchayat last year. Jaynangar gram panchayat under her able leadership has successfully shown that gram panchayats can play a positive role in the process of land acquisition and rehabilitation.

This award is given to Ms. Patra in recognition of her outstanding all round developmental work.

ASH NARAIN ROY
Director

INSTITUTE OF SOCIAL SCIENCES

Outstanding Women Panchayat Leaders Award

2012

Presented to

SHASHI KIRAN

on the occasion of

Women's Political Empowerment Day Celebrations

April 25, 2012, New Delhi

Ms. Shashi Kiran, Member, Zilla Parishad, Lahaul and Spiti, Himachal Pradesh, has been actively engaged in social and political life for many years. She had previously held the post of President, Mahila Mandal, for seven years in her district which gave her confidence to enter public life. She won the Zilla Parishad elections in 2011 on a general seat with a big margin.

Ms. Shashi Kiran played a key role in setting up self-help groups in her village. Her persuasive skills, perseverance and rapport with political leaders, government officials as well as community leaders resulted in many schemes and development projects coming her way.

She has taken pains to familiarize herself with government rules and regulations so as to take advantage of a plethora of development projects on health. She constantly fights for medical facilities and proper medical staff with the state government and state administration so that people living in difficult terrain and extreme climate can get proper medical treatment. She has also been instrumental in promoting local handicrafts as a means of sustenance for the people.

One of Ms. Kiran's significant achievements has been to get the "snow clearance" scheme included under MGNREGS. Lahaul and Spiti remain completely cut off for six to seven months from the rest of the country during the winter. She has also demanded one month's maternity leave for the working women in her area and helicopter services for all the patients to travel out of the district because of extremely severe climatic conditions.

The key to Ms Shashi Kiran's success is in her constant pursuit of the development agenda with a human touch. Her priority has been development and awareness among women. As such she has spent much time on getting approach roads in her district. Despite having to look after her home she has always attended panchayat meetings, be it Block level or Zilla Parishad level.

This award is given to Ms. Shashi Kiran for her outstanding leadership role.

ASH NARAIN ROY
Director

From left: Dr. Santosh Singh, Fellow, Institute of Social Sciences (ISS); Ms. Shashi Kiran, Member, Zilla Parishad, Lahul and Spiti, Himachal Pradesh; Ms. Manisha Gadve, Sarpanch, Kodoli Gram Panchayat, Maharashtra; Dr. George Mathew, Chairman, ISS; Mrs. Frederika Meijer, Representative, UNFPA, New Delhi; Shri V. Kishore Chandra Deo, Hon'ble Union Minister for Panchayati Raj and Tribal Affairs; Ms. Parbati Patra, Pradhan, Jaynagar Gram Panchayat, West Bengal; Ms. Puniben Chhanabhai Rajpara, Sarpanch, Mokasar Gram Panchayat, Gujarat; Ms. Anne Stenhammer, Regional Programme Director, UN WOMEN, New Delhi; and Dr. Bidyut Mohanty, Head, Women's Studies Unit, ISS.

Participants dancing with gusto

Ms. Shashi Kiran receiving the Award

Ms. Manisha Gadve receiving the Award

Ms. Parbati Patra receiving the Award

Ms. Puniben Rajpara receiving the Award

Ms. Vandana Prasad and Prof. Ritu Priya

Women in Governance

7
Panchayats and Universal Health Care*

Ritu Priya

Politics, Society and Health

Speaking on 'Health for All' always reminds me of what the Bairwa construction workers coming to Delhi from Rajasthan, belonging to an ex-untouchable caste group, had said during my long interactions with them over a decade ago. Discussing the changes in society and health services since Independence, they saw their own coming out of the curse of untouchability as the biggest gain and, therefore, 'equality' as the greatest 'morality'of the times since 1947. On the other hand, they saw 'commercialization' of all aspects of life as the biggest 'immorality' of the times. These were also the criteria they applied to their assessment of health services—being treated as equal to all other patients, and not being subjected to profiteering doctors—and on both these they found the present health services in the negative. They feel discriminated in a hospital as the rural and the poor get second class attention as against the urban middle class. Even in the government facilities that are meant to be free, the personnel have to be 'paid' and medicines, etc., have

* The keynote address.

to be bought from outside. If only President Obama of the USA could learn from and be allowed to build a healthcare system on this wisdom—that healthcare should not be about profits and should be available equally to all as a right, then the richest country of the world would solve one of its major problems today—how to ensure healthcare to all its citizens. I am saying this to point out that health and healthcare are not only matters in the hands of doctors or about having enough money, but about how we organize our society, about how social structures determine the conditions of people's lives and work, and thereby their health. Democratic politics and panchayats, which are meant to do inclusive decision-making about how to organize society to improve the lives of people are, therefore, central to any discussion on 'health for all'.

Virchow, a famous German doctor, pathologist, anthropologist, and politician, known for his advancement of public health, had said in 1848, "Medicine is a social science, and politics is nothing else but medicine on a large scale. Medicine, as a social science, as the science of human beings, has the obligation to point out problems and to attempt their theoretical solution: the politician, the practical anthropologist, must find the means for their actual solution.... The physicians are the natural attorneys of the poor, and social problems fall to a large extent within their jurisdiction". Thus doctors are expected to deal with the health problems of the poor who have the greatest ill-health and they can see their problems arising out of social conditions, therefore, doctors and all health care providers, have the responsibility to contribute to improving conditions of the poor and 'health care for all'.

Two Powerful Liberative Ideas: 'Women's Political Empowerment' and 'Health for All'

Women's political empowerment is a powerful idea today, with its history of over a century of struggle world-wide showing obvious results of improving women's opportunities and status in all societies. Unfortunately, in the present times of corporate globalization, the negative impact of commercialization of all dimensions of human life is impacting on even this extremely liberating idea. The gains of women's empowerment have been limited in terms of improving the well-being of women and all humans by the approach of exploitation of all possible resources for short-term gains. While women are getting empowered on one hand, on the other, they are being exploited by the commodification of their bodies, and by the promotion of a consumerist culture among them and their families. In such a situation, healthcare also becomes a casualty to the same distortions—commercialization, exploitation of people's suffering, exploitation of women's bodies especially through reproductive health-related unnecessary medical interventions. On the other hand, the lack of necessary medical services also adds to the suffering of people. Women's role as care givers in the family adds further to the impact on them of ill-health of all.

'Health for All' is, therefore, the second powerful idea that we are talking about today. This means, not only ensuring health services for all as per their requirement, but also all the basic needs that are necessary for ensuring a healthy body and mind for all human beings—adequate clean water, a sanitary environment, nutritious food in required quantity, housing and clothing, etc. But even these are not enough by themselves, also needed beyond these material necessities are a secure emotional environment, social support structures, and a healthy self-esteem and dignity in social relationships that are all essential for healthy human beings. That is also how the two ideas, women's empowerment and health for all, are closely inter-linked.

Ethics of Healthcare Practice

Since health problems are a major cause of human suffering, healthcare has been an important consideration of all social institutions interested in reducing suffering. However, it is individually, not an economically viable activity any longer, if it is practised ethically. It has to have the support of collective institutions that earn from other sources and develop collective forms of providing healthcare. That is why the government, the charitable/social responsibility bodies are essential to provide healthcare to all.

But when the primary purpose of healthcare providers becomes commercial gain, ethics are forgotten, and that is the negative tendency in medicine that has to be fought against. That is why we have to develop and strengthen the systems that can provide healthcare to the largest number of people, without consideration of the ability to pay, only provide according to the need to decrease suffering of the collective 'people'.

"Politics is short-term religion and religion is long-term politics", said Ram Manohar Lohia, the Indian socialist leader during our struggle for independence. We can interpret this to mean that the role of both is to do two things: decrease the suffering of people, and to control the debasing human tendencies and enhance the positive tendencies in society. Thus, it is not only the political processes and health service systems that are relevant for 'health for all', but also cultural institutions that create collective norms of entitlements, of public action and provide check mechanisms for people's greed.

Unfortunately, neither the system of doctors' services, nor the system of politics, nor of religion are actually performing these roles too well in the present times. In fact, they seem to be doing the reverse. This is not to say that there are no competent doctors, or politicians or religious persons; there are and that is why society is still running to the extent that it is functional in improving people's well-being. We have strong legacies of all these, and it is for us to strengthen the positives in all these social institutions for the betterment of all.

Several efforts in the past have helped to create systems to provide support against ill-health in our country, and the latest of these is the National Rural Health Mission (NRHM), the largest programme of making 'healthcare for all' in the world. So I will be speaking about the NRHM and the role of panchayats within it at some length. But before that, very briefly, I will outline the challenges it has to deal with.

The Background Context: The Two Costs of Modern Healthcare

Over the history of human societies, the knowledge of one's own body, of one's family's and community's health has most commonly been placed with women. The 'professsional' experts were often men, but their role was limited. However, the capacity and control to do something about health has, over the past two hundred years, been increasingly taken away from the hands of ordinary women and given to the experts. Modern medicine came into India with the British rulers and they used it to delegitimize the existing well-developed health culture, the folk practices and the more advanced knowledge of systems such as Ayurveda, Siddha and Unani that they were linked to. Since then, modern medicine has advanced much further and helped to relieve people's suffering, but it has now also reached a stage where it is producing as much harm as good, what Ivan Illich, a Latin American scholar who studied the negative impact of modern social systems, had called 'Medical Nemesis' in the 1970s. The USA is known on one hand for its effective medical services, and on the other, for the services being so expensive that they are out of reach for over one-fifth of even that rich country. The financial cost of medical care has increased so much that several companies, who by law had to provide healthcare for their employees, went bankrupt because of the medical bills they had to pay. But, besides the financial costs is the ill-health caused by the medical treatment, where every third hospital bed in the USA is treating cases of what is called 'iatrogenesis' (meaning—disease that I, the healer, have created). It is estimated to be the third biggest cause of death in the USA after heart disease and cancers.

And yet modern healthcare is also useful and necessary to reduce human suffering. Only, it must be as safe as possible, within the reach of all, and used as rationally as possible. What does rational healthcare mean? Given nature's own capacity to heal, doing something for treatment may not always be necessary or be able to do better than what nature does. Also, in dealing with health problems, various options are often available in the form of health improvement measures and choosing the most appropriate for the given conditions is what is rational. For instance, in the case of diarrhoeal diseases, we can improve water supply to decrease their occurrence, but once they occur, we can either give rice water or turmeric and jaggery boiled in water or oral rehydration solution made from a packet or an intravenous drip, with or without antibiotics. The rational choice in an individual case would be based on clinical assessment of the condition of the patient and the cause of the diarrhoea. At a collective public health level too, each of these must be available, but in most cases, the diarrhoea is known to be self-limiting and so only needs fluids to be taken in adequate quantity. The fluids easily available at home are then the most easily accessible and, therefore, the most rational. Taking unnecessary treatment, whether medicines, surgery or diagnostic tests, only increases the probability of suffering side effects due to these. In attempting to get treatment, people get indebted and fall into poverty or go into deeper poverty, in substantial numbers. Studies have shown that 5-10 per cent of households undertake 'catastrophic expenditures' every year in India, in what are seen as matters of life and death. And, while much of it may be necessary medical treatment, much of it is also unnecessary and due to irrational prescribing practices of the doctors.

The Role of Panchayats in Health

With this background, what is the role that panchayats and especially women panchayat members, can play in ensuring health for all? Constitutionally, some dimensions of health services are responsibilities of the central government and some of the state governments. The 73rd and 74th constitutional amendments placed primary level health services under the charge of the panchayat and municipal bodies.

This role is of crucial significance for improving health and healthcare. Panchayats can help plan and implement according to the need of the local people. Inter-sectoral coordination is possible at the local levels with mediation of the panchayat, and a supportive administration. They can play three important roles:

- Participate in implementation of health and health-related programmes and services.

- Monitor implementation of these programmes and services.
- Highlight needs not being addressed by the existing programmes and services and introduce them through innovative local planning.

With 36 lakh elected members in panchayats and nagar palikas, much should have happened. However, several studies have shown that there is a dual problem in the panchayats engaging in, or rather not engaging in, health-related work: Lack of interest on the part of panchayat members, and lack of value for their involvement by the health department and personnel. The panchayat members have a low interest in health for two reasons, one that there has till recently not been much fund allocation under their decision-making powers, and secondly that only the doctors and nurses are seen as competent to make decisions about health and so the lay members do not see a role for themselves. Unfortunately, the rise of the modern experts has led to medicalization of mindsets that takes the control out of people's hands and places it with the experts who use their power to exploit the people they are meant to benefit. Once we hand over that power, even the most well meaning doctor feels that they have all the knowledge and people do not know anything. Contrary to this is the understanding of social determinants of health that lay people know about much more than the MBBS trained doctors. Everyone knows that lack of cleanliness leads to illness; that 'food makes the body'; that what and how much work we do affects the state of the body. What herbs and food items can be used for home remedies, what foods can be harmful or useful at different stages in life and in the seasonal cycle over a year, these are also common knowledge. But when the doctors study the germs that cause disease, about the medicines that can fight the germs, about medicines that decrease blood sugar in diabetic patients, they forget this common knowledge. They see the patient only through the test reports and treatment only as medicines and operations. The good doctors are those who do not forget the basics, who give fewer medicines and get minimal tests done, who suggest changing ways of life in the community or workplace so that ill health is prevented and positive health is promoted. This is where government doctors generally do better than private doctors. The government doctors may be rude, they may have no time to give each patient because they have to see over 50 in one morning, but they also have little interest in prescribing unnecessary tests and medicines, if they do not have to be brought from outside. Studies have shown that the private doctors do much more irrational prescribing of tests and treatment than the government doctors. For the private sector, prescribing more tests, injections and medicines is seen as a way of increasing profits or making financially viable the investments in setting up their specialized facilities. In either case, however, the best and cheapest form of prevention and treatment is one that can be started at the earliest by the people themselves.

Therefore, if we have to keep the financial and ill-health costs of healthcare at a minimum, the government facilities must be strengthened and the people's own knowledge about home remedies, local foods, etc. documented, validated and promoted. Even the *Charak Samhita* (*Sutrasthana* 1/120-122) says that "*The goatherds, shepherds, cowherds and other forest dwellers know the medicinal herbs in the forest....*". Any harmful practices found can be discouraged. An 18 state study we undertook as part of the NRHM found that about 75 per cent of the knowledge of local medicinal plants and their uses in village households was correct by the AYUSH texts and principles. All over the country, people commonly knew the uses of *tulsi*, *neem*, *haldi* and pepper. Many more were locally known. Use of this knowledge has gradually declined because of the understanding that the doctor's medicine is best, and all this is backwardness. However, if you ask the doctors what they do when they have illness in their family, they also first try all these grandmother's remedies, or recommend homeopathy for their children. The high income countries like the USA and Europe have increasing use of these other systems, the World Health Organization estimating that over 70 per cent of the world's people use these other systems. Our better off more affluent people are also increasing their use, but our poor and rural are fast losing them. The commercial pharmaceutical companies and health tourism are fast expanding their products in these areas as well. However, the poor are being fed the idea that they must go to medical institutions for the more modern, more effective, more scientific medical care. The traditional science and art of health is likely to get lost in their non-commercialized forms if we do not take proactive steps to promote their rational practice.

Panchayats and NRHM

The National Rural Health Mission, announced in April 2005 and started in 2006, has attempted to undertake several steps to strengthen the public system of health services and to increase the role of communities in this. Its primary focus has been to make the existing health facilities—District hospitals, sub-district hospitals, Community Health Centres (CHCs), Primary Health Centres (PHCs) and sub-centres—provide better quality services and to attract more people to use them. This became necessary owing to the events in a long history of development of health services in the country. Till the 1980s, the government hospitals and doctors were the leaders of the profession and considered best by all. In the 1990s, with globalization of the economic policies, the private sector was given a boost and government expenditure in areas such as education and health, which are seen as 'non-productive', was decreased. The idea was promoted globally, that government services are poor in quality while the private ones are better. This led to doctors and patients moving away from the public services towards the private. However, by 2000, the negative impact of this was so widely felt that even the World Bank and US Congress had to openly acknowledge that 'the market' does not work in the case of health services and that government services are essential. That is how the NRHM was conceived, to increase government spending on health and strengthen government health services, including maternal and child health services.

It attempted to do so by:

- improving infrastructure, buildings, transport, drug supplies, etc.,
- increasing manpower, doctors, nurses, paramedics,
- decentralization with funds for local level spending and new management personnel supporting administration at all levels,

- mainstreaming AYUSH (an acronym for the codified systems of Ayurveda, Yoga and Natureopathy, Unani, Siddha, Sowa Rigpa and Homoeopathy) and revitalizing local health traditions, (i.e. folk practices and healers) and
- community participation for decentralized planning, monitoring and implementation.

Major achievements have been made on several fronts, such as increase by over 30 per cent MBBS doctors at PHCs and CHCs, 91 per cent more specialist doctors at CHCs, 102 per cent increase in nurses at PHCs ad CHCs, and 44 per cent more of ANMs (Auxiliary Nurse Midwives) in the government systems across states; increase in spending on health by 15-20 per cent per year, free drugs becoming available in facilities of almost all states much more than before; free transport for emergencies including delivery cases, etc. Over a thousand new sub-centres, over four hundred new PHCs and over a thousand new CHCs have come up. However, the achievements are clearly not enough to cater to the needs of all as yet. Much more strengthening of the system is still to be done.

Governance Structures and the Role of Panchayats

For decentralization, inter-sectoral coordination and community involvement, several structures have been created at all levels. At the highest national level, there is a Mission Steering Group that comprises the Ministers and/or Secretaries of all related ministries—Health and Family Welfare, Rural Development, Panchayati Raj, Human Resource Development, Women and Child Development, and the Deputy Chairman of the Planning Commission. Each state has a State Rural Health Mission (SRHM) and a State Health Society (SHS). The SHM is headed by the Chief Minister and members are the ministers and secretaries of all the related ministries and departments as well as 5-10 nominated members from elected representatives—MPs, MLAs, Chairman of Zilla Parishad (ZP), and municipal heads and 5 public health experts, i.e., elected representatives and technical experts. However, the SHS has only officials and management personnel as members.

In each district there is a District Health Mission (DHM) headed by the Chairperson of Zilla Parishad, for overall guidance to the NRHM in the district. It is to have the District Collector as the Co-Chair and Chief Medical Officer as the Mission Director. The District Health Society (DHS), headed by the District Collector or CEO of Zilla Parishad, as stated in the official documents of the NRHM, "will be responsible for planning and managing *all* health and family welfare programmes in the district, both in the *rural as well as urban* areas". Ensuring inter-sectoral convergence and integrated planning are the specific tasks for the Governing Body of the DHS. "However, the DHS is not meant to take over the executive functions of the Zilla Parishad, Urban Local Bodies (ULB) and district health administration. On the contrary, DHS is meant to provide the platform where the three arms of governance: the ZP, ULB and district health administration and district programme managers of NRHM sectors get together to decide on health issues of the district and delineate their mutual roles and responsibilities. The DHS may also be viewed as an addition to the district administration's capacity, particularly for planning, budgeting and budget analysis, development of *operational policy* proposals, and financial management". (see next page). This places the DHS secretariat (the District Programme Management Unit), with the district programme manager, data manager and accountant, as the additional management staff for the district health administration. They have, as experienced in most districts, added young blood with energy and capacities of computer processing and data handling, that have facilitated the functioning of the CMO of the district. However, the elected representatives, the panchayat, and the local communities must also be able to put their services to the best use for improving health and health services in the district.

Governance Structure in a District

District Health Mission and District Health Society

District Health Mission

Chairperson *Chairman, Zilla Parishad*

Co-Chair	District Collector/DM
Vice Chair	CEO Zilla Parishad
Convener	Chief Medical Officer/CDMO/CMHO/Civil Surgeon
Members	MPs, MLAs, MLCs from the district, Chair-persons of the Standing Committees of the Zilla Parishad, Project Officer (DRDA), Chair-persons of the Panchayat Samitis and Hospital Management Societies, District Programme Managers for health, PHED, ICDS, AYUSH, education, social welfare, Panchayati Raj, State representatives, representatives of MNGO/SNGO, etc.

District Health Society

The overall governance structure of the society may be as depicted in the diagram below.

Diagram 1: Governance Structure of the District Health Society

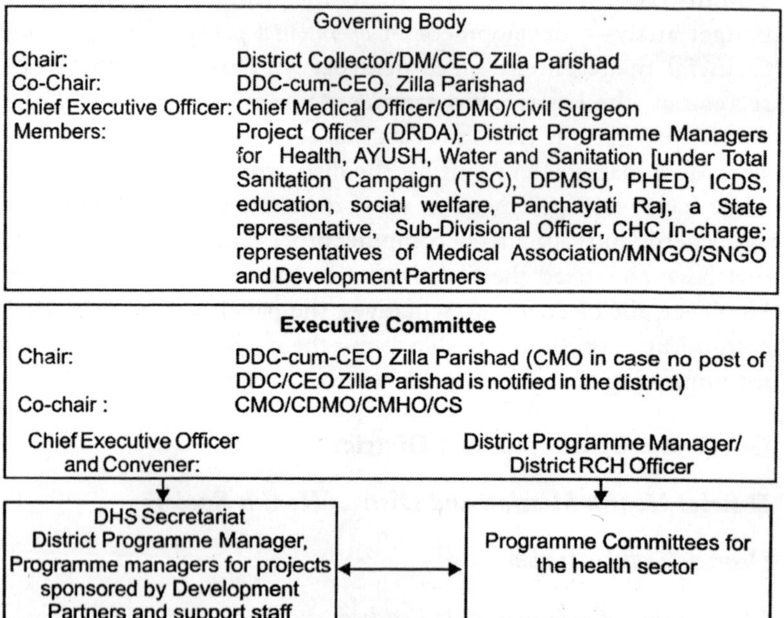

Source: NRHM website

The Rogi Kalyan Samiti (RKS)/Patient Welfare Society/ Hospital Management Society

Each of the health facilities are to register a separate society to manage the funds accruing to it for local expenditure from the NRHM. These have been variously termed in different states as the Rogi Kalyan Samiti or Patient Welfare Society or Hospital Management Society. Headed by the District Collector and with the Medical Superintendent as the Secretary, there is provision of two panchayat members to be nominated as members. In addition, NGOs and community members are also to be nominated members. Similarly, there are RKS for the CHC and PHC, with elected representatives of the panchayat as members at each level. These are all opportunities for the panchayats to assert their role in decision-making on behalf of the people. The fund available annually to each facility under the NRHM is: Rs five lakhs per district hospital, one lakh per CHC, fifty thousand per PHC and ten thousand per sub-centre.

However, what has been repeatedly observed is that the meetings are poorly attended by the panchayat members. One reason often offered has been that they have not been informed in time or well in advance so as to make themselves available for the meeting. The other complaint has also been that the DM or BDO and the Medical in-Charge always dominate the meetings and do not allow intervention by others, so what is the point of attending the meetings? It has also been documented that the expenditures undertaken by the RKS has not always been in the best interests of improving patient care for the majority. For instance, an expensive MRI machine was bought in a district hospital which only very few patients need for diagnosis, while there was no stethoscope and other basic equipment in the OPD and water supply was extremely inadequate. It needs to be seen how the panchayat members can assert themselves more and voice the priorities of the people.

One problem articulated by the ANMs who are incharge of the sub-centres and have the sarpanch as the co-signatory for the account of the NRHM funds at their disposal, has been of the male sarpanches troubling them each time they need their signatures. Unfortunately, this has led to many states creating procedures that allow them to bypass the elected representatives. The misuse of funds and/or disinterest of panchayat members is also the concern at higher levels and an argument given for why this other committee was formed even when the panchayats had village health committees. It was felt that a committee directly under the health department would be more effective than under the Panchayati Raj institutions. This is an issue for debate and discussion, for introspection by the panchayat members and health department alike. Is it only a turf battle for power between the departments/ministries or is there some element of truth in the arguments? Or is it a matter of stereotyping the negatives of elected representatives when the same arguments can be made for all official and medical personnel as well? However, rather than view it as an issue, the panchayat members can use the opportunity still available to them to demonstrate their interest in the people's welfare and health by proactively participating in all the activities and representing the view of the poorer majority of the village inhabitants at all levels of decision-making. Since women are the most affected and sensitive to such issues, such action can be expected most effectively from the women elected members.

The Village Health, Sanitation and Nutrition Committee

Each village is to have a Village Health, Sanitation and Nutrition Committee (VHSNC) consisting of the Accredited Social Health Activist (ASHA), ANM, AWW, 4-5 members of Self-Help Groups and a ward member elected to the panchayat, with representation of the SC/ST communities. There could be locally active NGO members as well. *This can become one of the most powerful women health collectives.*

This Committee is to get ₹ 10,000 every year to undertake work considered necessary to improve the health of the village residents. It is meant to prepare a village health plan and to undertake community monitoring of the health services. The VHSNC is also to be the forum for inter-sectoral coordination for health at the village level, i.e., action to be planned on improving water supply, sanitation, nutrition, healthcare and health awareness in an integrated way. Initially it was called the Village Health and

Sanitation Committee, and started working basically for immunization and promotion of institutional deliveries. With the high levels of malnutrition in the country, and the anganwadi under the ICDS being meant to deal with the problem of malnutrition, 'Nutrition' was added to the name of the committee so as to emphasize this component of its tasks.

In several places, the VHSNC fund has been used very effectively to bring the villagers together to improve environmental conditions in the village, or to provide money to poor families in times of medical emergency to enable them to reach hospital. In some villages, residents have been concerned about the malnutrition of children in the village and have collected money on their own to supplement the food being given at the anganwadi. However, in many states, the health department or SHS suggests that the funds are spent on something that is a gap in the medical equipment at the sub-centre or AW. This is not at all appropriate to the concept of the fund, and violative of the villagers' right to decision-making about the ten thousand allocated to the VHSNC.

A Village Health and Nutrition Day (VHND) is being organized every month in each village at the anganwadi. It is attended by the VHSNC members. It is to encourage immunization, ante-natal care, and growth monitoring of children as well as to serve as a monthly event that focuses on issues of health, so that villagers give it more attention. This mechanism has proved very effective in some places and is hardly being implemented in others. This is again an opportunity that panchayat members could use to strengthen health activities in the village.

The VHSNC is also to be the institution to facilitate the gram sabha in selecting the ASHA from among the women in the village. However, ASHA selection has, by and large, not been done through the gram sabha and VHSNC, in many places because the committee was not formed when the ASHA was selected, but generally because the ANM, Sarpanch and Medical Officer (MO) decided instead of the villagers being mobilized for this through the gram sabha.

Also, the role of the ASHA has primarily been as a mobilizer for immunization and institutional deliveries. However, in many places she has also been able to voice other felt needs of people, such as improving supply of rations in Koriya, Chhattisgarh. With the Village Health and Sanitation Committees (VHSCs) becoming Village Health, Sanitation and *Nutrition* Committees (VHSNCs), it is to be hoped that the ASHA will also pay greater attention to nutrition-related issues and assist the AWW in growth monitoring and identifying those who need special attention. Identifying unfulfilled basic needs of the community and mobilizing the VHSNC to deal with or voice demands for the rightful access to services should be seen as responsibility of the ASHAs.

Community Monitoring and Planning

The adoption of a comprehensive framework for community-based monitoring and planning at various levels under NRHM can be seen as an extremely positive development, which can place centre-stage community members and beneficiaries, community-based organizations and NGOs working with communities, along with panchayat representatives, allowing them to actively and regularly monitor the progress of NRHM interventions in their areas. Besides ensuring accountability, it could also promote decentralized inputs for better planning of health activities, based on the locally relevant priorities and issues identified by various community representatives.

However, this activity has hardly taken off in concrete terms. It was initially undertaken as a pilot in a few districts of 9 states. After the first round, it has been continued in only three states, and that too because of the proactive approach of the NGOs in these states who have been activists for people's right to health. However, its use in some states has been inspiring. *In Madhya Pradesh's Barwani district,* which is one of the poorest, with over two-third tribal population, the Community Monitoring and Jan Sunwais were able to bring about a significant improvement in the health services. Constant vigilance, occasional demonstrations and regular monitoring have yielded significant results in the health centres. They highlighted the corruption and negligence strongly, so that the administration was forced to acknowledge the problems, punish the guilty, and give adequate inputs to strengthen the infrastructure and its functioning. Corrupt doctors have been suspended, attendance of healthcare personnel has increased, the ambulance service started functioning, and basic essential medicines have been made available.

In Tamil Nadu, which has among the best government health services in the country, a group of NGOs have been working with the government, sensitizing the people and the public health doctors to use community monitoring as a tool to strengthen the health services from the people's perspective. The community's monitoring through surveys and Jan Sunwais is a feedback to the health administration and hospital in-charges about problems faced by the users of services so as to identify where the gaps are from the people's perspective. For the community, it becomes a tool to make them aware of what is their rightful expectation from the services. Dialogue generated between the two leads to greater mutual understanding of systemic problems and possible solutions to them.

However, these are rare examples and much more needs to be done to make community monitoring meaningful.

Similarly, village planning has got converted into an exercise of identifying the need for services that have to be planned for by the health personnel, such as how many children are expected to be immunized in the plan period, the number of pregnant women needing antenatal care and safe deliveries. It has not been used as a means of identifying the 'felt needs' of the community, then identifying the gaps in meeting those needs and finally planning for activities such as to fill those gaps. Thus, it has not even been envisaged as a real bottom-up planning, only as a means to make the top-down planning more effectively implemented.

In many states there is confusion between village planning and sub-centre planning. There is 10,000 for each of them, and that too adds to the confusion. Therefore, there is need for guidelines clarifying the objectives of the two as distinctly different entities; one is for what the villagers themselves will do using the funds as seed money and for inter-sectoral coordination for health-related work of different departments in the village, and the other is about what the health personnel posted at the sub-centre have to do in the village.

For the VHSNC to function effectively, an environment of solidarity in the village, of a collective responsibility towards all in the village, will be of great importance. This still exists in several parts of the country, but is getting lost rapidly. Can we decide that '*no one will go to sleep hungry in our village*' and that '*Let no one go without necessary treatment*'—'*Koi Bhookha Na Soye, Koi Bimar Gair-Ilaaj Na Rahe*'?

In Conclusion: Priority Tasks for Panchayat Members

Clearly, the NRHM has created greater possibilities to exercise control by people because of committees and societies that decide untied fund utilization. But generally the potential is unrealized. Often they have only token representation in the committee and even that is nullified by the flaunting of democratic norms in functioning of the committees.

However, there is also the problem of insufficient interest shown by panchayat members. This may have to do with their perception of health being a matter for doctors to handle and a lack of confidence in dealing with it themselves as lay people. This is a larger problem of over-medicalization of health and the loss of control by lay people to professional experts. This is a 'politics of knowledge' that the panchayat members must be enabled to fight against.

The NRHM provides an opportunity for this, by its strategy of mainstreaming of AYUSH and revitalizing of local health traditions. However, in many states, the AYUSH practitioners are being mainstreamed not the systems, i.e., the AYUSH doctors are being posted in PHCs where MBBS doctors do not go, and they are then expected to provide allopathic treatment, not their own system. And the LHT have received no attention at all as yet. The panchayat members must insist that the Indian Public Health Standard's requirement of cultivation of medicinal herbs and plants in the sub-centre and PHC compounds must be implemented. The AYUSH doctors posted at the PHC, CHC and District hospital too must be encouraged to use their own systems as far as possible and their medicines must be provided for by the system. The links between the local traditionally grown food crops and food patterns, that were linked to seasonal cycles of local food production and health should be examined and revived.

Problems have been faced by ANMs and ASHAs because of male sarpanches, so procedures have been devised to bypass the panchayats. Can the women panchayat members intervene in this and ensure that the honest ANMs and ASHAs are protected and the right of the panchayat to intervene in the local decision-making is not lost? Similarly, with almost half the children up to five years in our country being malnourished, can we try to ensure that what is provided for them through the anganwadis is not siphoned off? Is it not the most serious kind of inhuman crime to take away what is being provided as the right of hungry children? Can we create an environment where we can make people see that corruption in such areas of life and death—programmes and services dealing with food and healthcare—are just not acceptable? Contributing to these was the way to earn *punya,* robbing from it must mean a *paap* (sin) that society must not tolerate. As the examples of Badwani and Tamil Nadu show, there is something that can be done if there is a will and collective effort. This is the challenge for all the women panchayat members gathered here, and those not here as well.

Thus, what interested panchayat members can do within the present programme is: monitor implementation of NRHM and other health programmes and services; be involved in the VHSNC and Rogi Kalyan Samiti for planning for health at village, block and district levels, in each health centre and hospital; promote home remedies and other local health traditions, cultivation of herbal gardens and their use, use of AYUSH for prevention and treatment; promote the understanding that unnecessary use of medical technology is to be avoided—avoid unnecessary injections; avoid specialists unless essential; take closest and lowest level treatment first, then move up the ladder; and create an environment for 'no corruption' in food and healthcare-related programmes. This is a challenging list of tasks that will require dialogue and peaceful struggle against the prevailing powers in the health system, both public and private. But then this is necessary to ensure 'health for all'. That is the only way to enlist all possible support for the health and well-being of the powerless majority. Can your panchayat motto become: *'Koi Bhookha Na Soye, Koi Bimar Gair-Ilaaj Na Rahe'?*

"Our Panchayats
Our Future"

8

Orphaned Issues*

Vandana Prasad

Women's Health Beyond NRHM and the Potential Role of Women Panchayat Members

Women in panchayats have the dual responsibility of functioning as the general elected representatives of the people as well as representing the best interests of women in particular.

As far as the issue of women's health goes, the challenges are many, and while the NRHM takes some important steps related to women's health, specially in the context of maternity, it has also been inadequate to provide focus on many other women's health issues. This note seeks to highlight 'orphaned' issues in women's health, and suggests ways for the women panchayat members to take some action on them.

In policy and practice, as highlighted in the background note for this important meeting, (included in the proceedings) women have been treated in the utilitarian sense of beings who are primarily mothers, child carers or informal providers of care to other members of the society. Women's rights as an individual, over and above these

* After the keynote address, the Chairperson made certain remarks regarding the session.

roles, have not managed to attain centre-space either in policy or programmes. In fact, women interact with the health system in many important ways as listed below and all these have to be kept in mind:

1. As clients who should have the full spectrum of patients' rights, including the right to privacy, confidentiality, consent, right to records, quality of care and so on, and these are frequently denied.
2. As health workers with rights as workers to social security such as maternity entitlements, and decent wages. At a community level, there are over 6 lakh women working as ASHAs, about 2 lakh ANMs, about 28 lakh anganwadi workers and helpers and about 50,000 nurses at PHC level. This is a massive workforce of women in the country of about 40 lakhs. The rights of these women and their own health have to be considered, as well as the potential for empowerment and as a human resource.
3. As subjects for research: This is a new area where women are being identified for research on various drugs, vaccines and health-related
4. As participants in health programmes: there is an automatic assumption that women will provide their labour and time in the name of 'community participation' in health programmes, while men engage in economic activity. This notion can be empowering if the woman has choice, but often reinforces gender stereotypes of women not being engaged in economic activity and of women as prime carers in society. If women are allowed to be party to planning community participation, such as in the Village Health, Sanitation and Nutrition Committee (VHSNC), they would be able to exert enough influence to ensure that a fair balance is maintained between the participation of men and women. The panchayat leaders can play a critical role to examine the 'voluntary' roles women are expected to play in health programmes at the community level.

Apart from these, some specific health issues remain ignored and neglected by the health systems currently.

1. *Nutrition as a social determinant of health*: Women's nutritional status has been the source of much research and is exemplified by very high levels of anaemia, and low Body Mass Index (BMI). Women leaders must play a significant role as champions for adequate nutrition for women right through their life cycles. This implies fighting against the prototype of 'women to eat last and least' at the family level as well as systemic changes such as greater access to food security schemes. Women should be able to access PDS as individuals, and single women who do not appear in the excluded category should be automatically considered 'high priority' for food security schemes. The distribution of iron and folic acid through the public health system leaves much to be desired and the focus should be all women, not just women in the situation of maternity.
2. *Violence against women*: While this is well accepted theoretically as a major health issue affecting women, there is poor acknowledgement of the issue at community level, within programmes as well in health policy. The women panchayat leaders can play a major role in bringing the issue out of its invisibility as well as facilitating supportive community action on this issue.
3. *Mental health issues*: Depression and anxiety is a common feature of women's health complaints but the current programmes for mental health are very weak on the ground with poor integration within the NRHM. Again, the women panchayat leaders can play a major role in bringing the issue out of its invisibility as well as facilitating supportive community action on this issue.
4. *Occupational health problems of women*: Many women are engaged as labourers in the informal sector and suffer from various occupational health problems. There is currently no programme to account for these and ensure measures to prevent and manage such health problems, for example,

ailments related to the lungs from *bidi* making, skin diseases from agricultural work, etc.

5. *Cancers related to women*: Breast and cervical cancer are common in terms of relative incidence of malignancies but there are very poor provisions for screening and management. Advocacy is needed at every level to create a demand for services related to these.
6. *Menstrual and post-menopausal problems*: As life expectancy improves, many more women are to be found in the post- menopausal ages in our villages, with attendant serious problems of osteoporosis, dysfunctional bleeding, etc. Since the RCH programme is highly focused on women in the reproductive age group of 15-49, this group escapes the attention of the health system and gets very poor service.

Of course, there are gender-related issues in all the health programmes being run currently, such as the programmes for malaria and tuberculosis, but the aforementioned issues are truly orphaned at the moment.

Women panchayat representatives along with the *Mitanins* (ASHAs) in Chhattisgarh have played an important role in highlighting health issues for the whole community as part of a process called 'Swasthya Panchayat' in which each panchayat is given a report card based on its health achievements. This also forms the basis of village health plans, which can become the vehicle of addressing some of the orphaned issues outlined above. Such participatory processes at village level can be led by women panchayat representatives with the help of facilitating agencies such as local friendly civil society groups. If these become the basis of regular village health plans; the goal of decentralized planning within the public health system can be established to some extent while we continue demands for devolution of finances and administrative powers. However, all these processes require some minimum capacity building, preparation and facilitation for them to be successful.

Women panchayat leaders can play a significant part in ensuring that women's health issues are seen in a comprehensive way without minimizing them to the phases of child bearing and rearing. However, for this, they have to firstly empower themselves with information and capacities so that they can challenge the current paradigm and demand a more comprehensive approach to women's health issues.

> *Being a man or a woman has a significant impact on health, as a result of both biological and gender-related differences.*
>
> World Health Organization
> http:www.who.inl/topics/womens_health/en/

9

Panchayats and Health

K.B. Saxena

The enactment of the 73rd amendment to the Constitution is a landmark in the evolution of Indian polity and a policy measure of historical significance in more senses than one. It ushered in local governance institutions below the level of the state government as a third-tier of democratic structure. It transformed erstwhile dormant and weak institutions into constitutional bodies with defined jurisdiction, powers and functions, elective process of composition and autonomy from interference. It at once opened up space for millions of political leaders from grassroots level to emerge and created a huge potential for political mobilization of people in a manner never witnessed before on issues touching their daily lives. The revolutionary character of this move lay in providing 33 per cent reservation for women besides representation for SCs/STs according to constitutional provisions. This provision broke in one stroke the shackles imposed by the patriarchal social order characteristic of most communities in the country of whatever religious persuasion (barring some communities in Meghalaya and Kerala) which subordinated women to male domination and governed their role by cultural norms defined by it. This mandatory representation of women neutralized their political exclusion practised by all governance systems—formal and informal including those which provided greater participation to them in social and productive activities. Lakhs of women who never moved out of the narrow confines of their social environment, house, family, circle of relations, etc., and approached the external world only through their male kin were catapulted to a leadership role. This opportunity provided them with an opportunity to shed their inhibitions and deal with men on an equal footing. This elevation of status in society has generated tremendous self-confidence in them to face life and articulate their interests. They have become part of the governance system—dealing with officials and taking decisions rather than remaining petitioners seeking benefits and justice from them. The officials now treat them with courtesy and consideration rather than with condescension. Their elective position also enhances their status in society and enables them to be assertive in decision-making in the family. This opportunity also empowers them to carry out much needed development work in their village and reach benefits of programmes to the people. Women of their constituency particularly expect them to raise their problems and have them addressed. The revolutionary potential of this measure cannot, therefore, be overemphasized.

Health and Development

Health is the foundation of all development. Good health of the people is a precondition for economic growth, enhanced productivity and progress of the country as also for personal advancement, prosperity and happiness. Good health of the people is an asset which is vital for any nation wishing to make its presence felt at the global level. People with ill health are a liability to their family and to society. They can neither participate in economic activities for a dignified survival nor can contribute to societal good. Good health depends on a number of factors which include economic security, good quality of life and access to health services. The country is faced with a critical situation in respect of all three. Many people face unemployment, insecure work and, therefore, suffer from food and income insecurity, impoverishment and poor quality of life measured in terms of access to housing, drinking water, sanitation, education and health services. The health status of people provides a very grim picture—extremely high level of malnutrition and under-nutrition, continued high level of maternal mortality and infant mortality, increasing burden of both communicable and non-communicable diseases. This is combined with inadequate availability of public health services, high cost of healthcare, differentiated access to and poor quality of healthcare. Even the limited services which are available do not reach them, particularly in the backward and remote pockets of rural areas. The marginalized social groups face social barriers too in access to health services. Women's health is the most neglected dimension because it fails to get the desired attention in the patriarchal set-up of the family. This is compounded by women's low awareness about what constitutes ill-health. They also face constraints in approaching health providers owing to distance, economic factors, and lack of privacy. The current public health set-up at the primary healthcare (PHC) level suffers from absence of doctors/paramedics, non-availability of medicines, limited nature of services, inadequate supportive amenities and facilities, and difficulties of access in terms of distance and transport. In the absence of effective linkages with secondary and tertiary healthcare, it fails to tackle the complex health complaints which people face. Above all, non-existence of a credible mechanism of social accountability of health service providers deprives the local people of the required forum and space to seek their reform and improvement. The private sector healthcare is of uneven quality and unregulated. The good quality private sector healthcare is of high cost and out of reach for most people. Unqualified practitioners of varying degrees service a large part of the private health sector.

A larger number of poor, therefore, end up by accessing these service providers with considerable risk to their life and health. Despite inputs of additional resources and programmes, currently under the National Rural Health Mission (NRHM), no significant improvement has been registered in the public health system. It has now been recognized that the control of Panchayati Raj Institutions (PRIs) over local public health institutions and services is the only effective mechanism to improve the healthcare delivery and make health services more responsive to the needs of the people.

Health is one of the 29 subjects assigned to the PRIs. This provides a legitimate area of intervention by the PRIs to achieve the objective of reaching healthcare to all the needy people. It is, therefore, necessary that the elective members of the gram panchayats–the lowest unit of PRIs are made aware of the tremendous potential of their role in improving the health of people in their jurisdiction.

Challenges before Panchayat Members Information on Health Issues

Women panchayat members face huge challenges in discharging their role in matters relating to health particularly of women and children. The first challenge is to acquire necessary knowledge about health problems, structure of health services, preventive health measures, availability of curative healthcare facilities, particularly under different disease control programmes, which provide treatment/cure, constraints which people (particularly women) face in accessing them and how these difficulties can be removed. Imparting health education to women panchayat members, therefore, constitutes the first major step in building their capacity for this purpose. This education should consist of the following components.

- What are the major health problems of the people, particularly those of the women and children in the area? This should include the perception of people themselves about their illness and their health-seeking behaviour. This is important because people from the poor strata tend to ignore their ailments unless it severely constrains their capacity to work. Women across classes are more prone to do so because of social constraints, shyness, lack of attention from the family, pressure of work, etc. But these complaints may develop into more serious diseases if not treated in time. Therefore, no health-related complaint should be ignored. One dimension of this education is, therefore, to help people articulate their health problems and seek a doctor's advice on them.

- The second dimension of this education would focus on factors which give rise to health-related complaints, their implications for the future if not treated in time and what treatments are available for giving relief to those suffering from them.
- The third dimension of education should relate to available health services and the need for their utilization. For example, the most common health problems of younger women relate to their reproductive health. For women in pregnancy, there is provision for ante-natal check up, for institutional delivery, post neo-natal check up for health of the infant, supply of iron folic tablets for treating anaemia, etc. under *Janani Suraksha Yojana* (JSY). A woman health worker or Accredited Social Health Activist (ASHA) is available in the village to help access these services. The anganwadi worker is available for providing nutrition and health-related services to children besides running supplementary nutrition programmes. Panchayat members should mobilize women to avail of these services and liaise with health workers – ASHA, ANM, Anganwadi Worker (AWW) for sorting out any problems which they encounter in accessing them. However, women's health issues go beyond maternal morbidity and mortality and include abortion, Reproductive Tract Infections, Sexually Transmitted Diseases including HIV-AIDs besides communicable and non-communicable diseases which are common to both men and women. There are disease control programmes for communicable and non-communicable diseases. The RCH programme covers abortions and RTIs. A woman experiencing any such complaint can approach ANM of the sub-centre through ASHA who can refer the case to the concerned programme specialist for investigation and treatment. The most commonly articulated of women's health complaints include non-specific fever, acidity, weakness, respiratory ailments, etc. These symptoms need to be investigated so as to locate their causes and prescribe treatment. Women's

health is also greatly impacted by violence, physical and mental inflicted on them in the family. Psychiatric treatment and social counselling may be required in such cases.

- The fourth dimension of this health education is detection of diseases—particularly communicable diseases such as TB, malaria, leprosy, HIV, etc. Then there are water-borne diseases such as diarrhoea, vomiting, and jaundice. The increasing incidence of non-communicable diseases includes diabetes, hypertension, cardiovascular complaints and cancer. There are also diseases caused by nutritional deficiency, polluted environment, unsafe working conditions and hazardous occupations. Physical disability at birth may occur due to various factors—lack of nutrition, wrong medication, accidents, and inability to access health services in time. It is necessary to have some knowledge about the most common symptoms of these diseases so that they can be investigated at the earliest stage by referral to a doctor. The knowledge should also include preventive steps for a disease-free life—clean environment, regulated lifestyle, healthy food habits and timely check-up, etc., so that panchayat members can, within the limits of their status and power promote them. The local ANM at the sub-centre can help in detection of diseases at the earliest stage and refer the case to the specialist physician for further investigation. The panchayat members should guide the people, particularly women, not to ignore these complaints and go in for an early check-up so that timely treatment can prevent complications, catastrophic illness and disability. Most of these diseases are treatable and, in many cases, the treatment including medicine is free. The panchayat members should also mobilize people not to consult quacks or untrained health providers as it can lead to irreparable damage to health and sometimes even risk to life.
- The fifth dimension of this education is regarding the social determinants of health. Good health cannot be promoted

by merely providing easy access to comprehensive curative health services. Most of ill health can be prevented by desirable social conditions such as income security along with social protection for old age and disability, a quality of life which provides access to safe drinking water, sanitation and ventilated housing and a clean environment, safe conditions at the workplace which prevent damage to health and risk to life and regulate conditions of work. In the case of women, social relations within the family, i.e., the home environment is extremely important—lack of stress, equality of treatment in food distribution, access to health services, share in decision-making and work and responsibility in the family. There are programmes for poverty alleviation, provision of wage/self-employment, drinking water, sanitation and housing. Labour laws seek to regulate working conditions and protect the interest of the workers. The challenge is for the needy and disadvantaged persons to access these programmes. Panchayat members have to be imparted information and knowledge about them and institutional arrangements for their implementation and how they can be accessed. As for the social environment at home, no formal education is necessary as the problems are a part of the daily lives of people everywhere. The education in this regard should focus on the health impact of the social environment and legal and preventive steps that can be taken to deal with certain situations. NGOs and activists dealing with these issues can impart this education and undertake social counselling not merely of the affected women but also the concerned members of the family whose behaviour impacts their mental health.

- The sixth dimension of this education should extend to local health traditions—homemade remedies (grandmother's prescriptions) and the use of herbal remedies, etc. Most of these health practices are time-tested, risk free, and can be safely used when the complaint is not serious. In fact, overwhelmingly large numbers of people

> in rural areas and some even in the urban areas use them as they cannot afford the time and expenses to access public health services located at a considerable distance and private healthcare because of its cost. These practices are still the mainstay of healthcare in interior tribal areas where neither public nor private healthcare is available. This knowledge is transmitted from generation to generation in the family and society. There are also other traditional health practitioners some of which if accessed without seeking advice from the qualified medical practitioners may entail risks to health. Requisite knowledge about such risky practitioners is essential so as to avoid falling a victim or prey to them. Panchayat members should collect information about such risky practices and help spread awareness among their constituents about their dangers to health. They should arrange a qualified doctor from the public health facility to explain these dangers. Where there is doubt whether an existing practice is sound or risk-prone, expert advice of a local doctor should be obtained. But established and recognized systems of alternative medicine such as Ayurveda, Unani, Yoga, Siddha, Naturopathy and Homeopathy when practised by qualified practitioners are safe. There are some diseases which are best cured by these systems without adverse side effects. This knowledge should also be briefly extended to them. These systems are cheaper in cost, easy to access, and administer and harmonize with cultural mores and lifestyle of people.

If this major challenge is faced by acquisition of health education and its dissemination among the people, half the battle for promoting good health can be won. Panchayat members can mobilize health functionaries to interact with people on a periodic basis to spread this awareness. They should particularly mobilize women health providers, in the PHC (lady doctor if available), to interact with women who would be far more open and comfortable in communicating their problems to them and seeking their advice on addressing them.

Reproductive and Child Health Maternal Mortality

The second major challenge relates to achieving improvements in reproductive and child health. The country faces unacceptable levels of infant mortality, maternal mortality, underweight and stunted children, malnutrition and under-nutrition, anaemia both in the male and female population. Maternal mortality is caused by failure to have a regular ante-natal check-up and follow-up with prescribed medication and non-institutional delivery where complications cannot be treated and safe delivery cannot be ensured. It may also occur due to non-availability of requisite health services at an easily accessible distance for dealing with complications. The mother and infant face grave risk if the pregnant woman suffers from malnutrition and is unable to afford requisite nourishment and rest. Available health services under NRHM take care of these contingencies. What is required is to ensure that the pregnant women use these services and social, economic, and cultural barriers which prevent such utilization in time are eliminated. The entire family of the pregnant woman has to be motivated to ensure that this happens. If certain constraints in the availability of services—doctors, medicines and investigation aids are lacking in health services infrastructure, panchayat members have to raise the matter in the panchayat and at higher levels to get them. They should hold local health providers accountable for their inability to provide these services satisfactorily. They can mobilize the head of the panchayat to take up the matter with the higher level of health officials and other PRI members for addressing these shortcomings.

In some areas, transport is not available to take women in labour to the hospital. Panchayat members have to mobilize the village community to help in the short run by using a tractor/rickshaw/bullock cart, etc., in emergency situations besides raising the issue with officials at block/district levels so that with proper convergence of available programmes some transport facilities are arranged as a long-term measure.

Infant Mortality

Infant mortality is caused by several factors ranging from lack of proper nutrition during pregnancy and after delivery, failure to have regular ante-natal check-up, unsafe delivery, neglect in immunization and post neo-natal check-up, environmental factors leading to poor quality of life specifically reflected in unavailability of or lack of access to safe drinking water, sanitation, and clean air. Development programmes are available to address these issues. Panchayat members can contribute to reduction in the level of infant mortality by inducing mothers to access services and benefits of these programmes and sorting out constraints which stand in the way of this access. They should encourage women and their husbands to take preventive steps and consult the doctor at the earliest if illness occurs. Necessary health education of the women and also of men is necessary for this purpose. The local ASHA and ANM can help them in this task.

Underweight Children

The phenomenon of underweight children and stunted growth is largely due to severe malnutrition of both the mother and the child. Anaemia too results from insufficient and nutritious food, over-exertion and poor quality of life. This may result from poverty of the household and inadequate purchasing power caused by unemployment/under-employment, low income and uncertainty of work. The untreated diseases may also cause physical debility of a permanent nature. Here too, the task of panchayat members is necessary. They should ensure reach of the relevant programmes to the needy beneficiary and help eliminate bottlenecks in accessing them. Lack of nutrition for the mother and the girl child may also result from social practices and cultural norms, which discriminate in food distribution within the family by giving priority and a larger share to the male head and male child. Similar discrimination between the male and female child operates in access to education and other avenues of advancement. This needs to be countered by appropriate social mobilization.

Panchayat members, particularly women, should compete with one another in demonstrating that their ward has the healthiest women and child population. This would convey the right signals to other panchayats.

Discriminatory Practices against the Girl Child

The third major challenge to women members of the panchayat are the issues of low child sex ratio, sex-selected abortion, killing and abandonment of girl children and child marriages. This is the most difficult challenge to tackle which would test the ingenuity, patience, courage and strength of the panchayat members. All these social practices result from the patriarchal social order which values a male child, devalues women's contribution to the family, regards a girl child as a liability and systematically discriminates against her in the family in provision of education, attending to their health problems and fulfilling their aspirations. Difficulties in addressing these issues should not be ignored as taking a stand upfront would bring them in confrontation with the male leaders (and sometimes elderly female members) of the community and they may face ostracism, hostility and even worse treatments. They may not even be supported by their own family members who may put pressure on them to resign from their elective position or create various obstructions in attending to their work. But this is a challenge which women members must accept in order to secure a future of dignity, equality and freedom for women. They should devise a strategy of addressing these issues keeping in view their limitations. They should first win the battle within the family through appropriate but gradual conscientization not losing heart at the failure to get a positive response. They should identify more enlightened members of the village community with whose help this task should be pursued and who could be in the forefront to deal with community leaders (usually male). Necessary help of the concerned government officials should also be sought to tackle persistent resistance. They should ensure that the schemes to benefit the girl child reach the concerned families. They should organize functions, *melas* (fairs), periodic gatherings, where strengths and achievements of girl children are highlighted. The battle will certainly be long. But they should not give up in the face of resistance and hostility because the hold of patriarchal social values is gradually loosening. The future will be with them because the enlightened people in the country would be on their side in this movement of revolutionary social change.

Convergence of Programmes

The fourth major challenge which women panchayat members face is convergence of programmes which contribute to good health—access to safe drinking water, sanitation, housing, clean environment, nutrition, housing fuel wood and fodder, employment, safe conditions at the work site, etc. Various programmes exist which provide these entitlements. These programmes are administered by different ministries and departments in the government. But these programmes are implemented independently of one another and, therefore, fail to get converged in their delivery to the people who need them most so as to make an impact on the health and well-being of the population in an area. The dispersal of responsibility over several agencies makes convergence of these programmes at the top level difficult. Panchayats are the natural and the most effective space for achieving convergence since beneficiaries of all these programmes come from the villages. The test of having achieved convergence is that the entitlements/services or facilities should reach in a holistic manner so that ill health can be prevented and good health can be promoted. There is a village level health and sanitation committee under NRHM, which promotes convergence relating to drinking water, sanitation and health. It has also been expanded to include nutrition. The NRHM provides for preparation of a Health Plan by the three tiers of the PRIs. The first stage of this exercise is the preparation of a village Health Action Plan. The plans of the constituent villages have to be amalgamated to form a Panchayat Health Action Plan. While preparing this plan, the women panchayat members should focus on convergent delivery of programmes dealing with relevant social determinants in an integrated manner so as to promote good health. They should collectively strive to ensure that different functionaries of line departments visit the panchayats and intimate the members on how convergence can take place and help them in incorporating this design in their plan to achieve this objective. The District Health Plan should factor in all the plans prepared by the sectoral agencies dealing with these determinants and lay down mechanisms by which each agency would deliver its programmes in the village in a specified manner so as to achieve convergence. Thereafter, collective pressure should be built up on the higher level officials for organizing training of functionaries of various converging departments and providing clarity to them on their roles and responsibilities. This task is difficult as government agencies work in isolation and compartments. It requires a considerable effort to bring them on one platform and motivate them to work together. The task of panchayat members is to identify sectors which need to converge and where (individual/group/area) so that factors affecting health are addressed. Periodic monitoring by panchayats of the impact of these measures would help in building up a mechanism of accountability.

Promotion of Good Health

The sixth major challenge is to promote good health among people in your area. This involves organizing health education campaigns particularly targeting children, adolescents and women (especially in the reproductive age group) which focus on influencing people about their lifestyle and behaviour in matters which have a bearing on health. This involves avoidance of risks such as use of tobacco, alcohol, drugs through a heightened sense of health awareness, regular physical activity, selection of proper food, prompt consultation with the healthcare providers in the case of health related complaints, maximization of nutritional benefits from locally available foods, micro-nutrient supplementation, fortification of salt with iron and iodine, regular preventive health check-ups in schools and workplaces, dissemination of information on lifestyle choices, maintaining a clean environment with proper waste disposal practices, avoidance of stagnant water, proper ventilation in the house and use of smokeless *chulhas,* etc. Panchayats can take a lead in organizing these campaigns in their area culminating in the village health *mela* where token awards can be given for the best performance to an individual/family as an encouragement.

Enhancing Community Participation

The seventh major challenge lies in enhancing community

participation in planning, implementation, monitoring and evaluation of health programmes—rather the entire range of development programmes as they have a direct or indirect bearing on people's health. The community participation is already enshrined in the National Rural Health Mission (NRHM). But it has to go beyond its limited design and framework. Panchayats are assigned functions and responsibilities relating to other development programmes too and provision of good health is dependent on convergent action of several of them. The community mobilization should seek to remove in people the fear of authority, develop courage in them to articulate grievances, hold local officials responsible for failure to deliver services, demand compliant action in respect of entitlements and maintain social cohesion with a view to building continuous pressure till the complaints are addressed and the objectives are achieved. The community mobilization should also focus on issues where action has to be taken by the community itself and strive to see that it happens. It should particularly make efforts to ensure that the problems and interests of weaker sections—SCs, STs, women, minorities and physically challenged are fully reflected in collective action. The community mobilization should encourage open dialogue, free articulation of views, frequent and transparent consultation, sorting out differences through consensus building and accommodation so that greater participation is induced and achieved.

Constraints in Discharging Role of Cultural Values of Patriarchy

Women panchayat members face tremendous constraints in discharging their role. They are still overwhelmed by restraints and diktats of the patriarchal social order. Many women elected representatives are not allowed to attend meetings unless accompanied by a male family member. Worse, they are represented by their husbands or male kin in proxy participation. Unfortunately, the officials do not object to it and it is accepted as the social reality which must be accommodated even if at the cost of legality and ethics. Their male relatives dictate the views to be expressed and decisions to be taken. This defeats the empowerment which the provision of reservation intended to promote. Many of them are forced to consent to this arrangement because the cost of defiance or confrontation is high. Some of them even internalize this subordination as they suffer from inhibitions and fear of stigmatization. Where they do participate despite these constraints, they face discrimination and taunts of their male colleagues and, in some cases, are pressurized to agree to some decisions which they may not have taken in an environment free from fear and hesitation. Such women have to be helped strategize how slowly they can wrest freedom and autonomy even in the prevailing social milieu without unacceptable risk to themselves or their families. Some of those who succeed in breaking this barrier could be asked to assist/guide them in this process for which specially focused training/ consultation programmes should be organized with the help and assistance of women social activists and NGOs.

Low Level of Participation in the Gram Sabha

Lack of women's participation in gram sabha meetings has emerged as a major constraint. Even the attendance in gram sabha meetings by men members is very low across the country. But women's attendance is negligible if not non-existent. Several reasons may explain this phenomenon ranging from pressure of work at home, discouragement from male family members, lack of motivation, fear of criticism from village elders and a faith that, in any case, the male kin attending these meetings would raise issues concerning the village problems and that of women in particular. The situation of poor attendance does not change even where the head of the panchayat is a woman. Besides, even if a few women do occasionally attend meetings, they rarely speak or are not that articulate on specific issues related to them. The latter factor may be due to shyness and culturally embedded reluctance to speak at a gathering dominated by male folk. The result is that women-related issues rarely get raised. Thus, women's reluctance to raise their health problems in the family is compounded by absence of a mode of collective articulation in the representative body like the gram sabha or even the panchayat. The elected women members of panchayats can break this vicious circle by holding informal women exclusive meetings in the village where women would feel free to attend and speak their minds and could be encouraged to talk about health and other issues which have a bearing on their collective interests. After gathering this feedback, these issues can be raised in the gram sabha or other appropriate forum by the women panchayat members. Further, women panchayat members should encourage other women to attend gram sabha meetings, perhaps in a group, where they would feel more at ease. There is also no reason why women panchayat members cannot requisition a separate gram sabha meeting for discussion exclusively on women related issues of health and development where women alone would attend. The women panchayat members also have a duty to assert that schemes or decisions related to any sector which may have an adverse impact on women should not be pursued or should be modified to accommodate their interests before they are implemented. The point being stressed is that the elected women members must ensure optimum women's participation in a democratic forum to slowly neutralize the constraints imposed by the cultural norms of the patriarchal social order. Women social activists and NGOs working with women have an important role in breaking the gender barrier in participation.

Reluctance to Devolve Powers and Resources

PRIs in general face the crippling constraint that most state governments have been reluctant to devolve functions, functionaries and funds to them in consonance with the requirements of the 73rd amendment. Health is one of the subjects assigned to the PRIs. There is no reason why control over healthcare institutions PHC/sub-centres should not be entrusted to the panchayats and higher level health institutions to Block/District panchayats. In the absence of this devolution, PRIs cannot address the health concerns of their constituents. The service providers would hardly bother to act on the suggestions and directions issued by the PRIs unless they are directly accountable to them. At present, they feel accountable to their bureaucratic superiors. This is an issue which concerns the entire PRI set-up and not merely the women panchayat members and has to be agitated through collective mobilization of the PRIs as a whole at the state level. They would have the support of the central government in this endeavour if ever such a mobilization is accomplished. But women panchayat members can exert pressure in various tiers of PRIs that realization of Millennium Development Goals (MDGs) relating to health-reduction in IMR, MMR, etc. would not be possible unless the local PRI has control over health services and health providers. This realization already exists in the central government and the Plan Document and NRHM guidelines do advocate effective decentralization. What is required is mobilization of PRI members across the tiers and across the districts. This is a huge political space waiting to be tapped by political and civil society formations.

Training and Capacity Building

There is no doubt that the expectations from women panchayat members to play the desired role in planning and execution of health related measures would require substantial training and capacity building besides conscientization to loosen the hold of the patriarchal social order. They would need to be imparted knowledge of health issues, programmes and structures, awareness of the process of functioning of health institutions and how they can be used to get the requisite services. The shyness, hesitation and fear in them have to be slowly removed. They have to be guided on how they can discharge their role as a public functionary without sacrificing their responsibilities in the family and how they should become a role model to women constituents of their area in this regard.

Catering to Constituency

This capacity building would require support in terms of resources and a dedicated programme with requisite focus. The Ministry of Panchayati Raj provides some resources for this purposes. Besides, different central government development programmes also have a component of training. This includes NRHM, Right to Education

(RTE), drinking water (DW), sanitation, and the Mahatma Gandhi National Employment Guarantee Scheme (MNREGS), etc. All these resources can be pooled for taking up a composite capacity building programme. Here too, women panchayat members can exert pressure on the concerned implementing officials of different agencies to arrange training programmes for capacity building in an integrated manner. They can also articulate requirements for such an integrated programme suiting their specific needs.

Women panchayat members not merely represent women voters of their constituency but the entire population and would, therefore, have to take up issues of men (young and elderly) as well besides those of women and children. They should be able to show that they can represent interests of all social groups and both the sexes and pursue an integrated development agenda for the village far more effectively and equitably than men have been able to do. The success in achieving this goal would decisively break the cultural barrier against women imposed by the patriarchal society and would enable them to get their support for winning elections in future.

Agreed Agenda for Action

The collective meets of the type ISS organizes annually provides a unique space for inter-personal and social interactions among panchayat members. It provides a mechanism through which women panchayat members discuss among themselves issues outlined above as also many others relevant to their specific concerns, exchange experiences of successes and failures, gather new ideas and build up friendships, and camaraderie. It is hoped that they will use such occasions to work out an agreed agenda which they wish to pursue in their respective areas.

> "An acceptable level of health for all the people of the world by the year 2000, can be attained through a fuller and better use of the world's resources, a considerable part of which is now spent on armaments and military conflicts."
>
> —*Alma Ata Declaration on September 6-12, 1978.*

10

AYUSH as an Alternative System of Treatment

Madhulika Banerjee

The importance of Ayurveda, Unani, Siddha and Homoeopathy (AYUSH) systems is being better understood and appreciated again—because they are simple, effective, possible to produce cheaply and belong to the everyday life and culture of people. These are qualities that can enable people everywhere, especially those in rural areas in India who have been dependent on state and private agencies to provide healthcare. Which is not to say that the responsibility of the state is to be any less, but if the representatives of the people at the lowest level know and understand what exactly their healthcare needs are, they can demand accordingly from the state—whether AYUSH or modern medical care.

One of the most important legacies that women have carried has been that of being the carers in their families and communities. While this has made women mainly confined to a role in the personal space, it has a value that can now be very relevant once they start taking positions of power in the public space as well. The value lies in the fact that women have very sound and detailed knowledge of two very important aspects of life and health—nutrition and medicine. I am going to discuss the latter. People in rural communities know the flora around them very intensively and women are required to make it both nutritionally and medicinally available. While this is true for much of the non-modern world, in India, an abiding approach to both these aspects is that they are related, indeed, food is medicine up to a great point in the health of people. Further, plants, foods and the human body are understood in the same terms, i.e., of humoral properties. The maintenance of health and sickness is understood in terms of keeping a balance in the body and between the body and food. 'Ordinary' women have been the informal repositories of medical knowledge from one generation to the next, in terms of the responsibilities that have been envisaged for them. Since their knowledge came from their immediate context, it had applicability and relevance to it, thus also constituting an important part of the 'local culture' that people identified and were comfortable with. This basic relationship between women and medical knowledge is what is relevant to understanding the linkage between AYUSH and women in panchayats.

Apart from women, local health traditions are practised by all kinds of traditional healers who specialize in medicines derived from local flora, even fauna. These healers do not necessarily hail from any lineage of textual learning of Ayurveda but usually have a narrow range of very effective treatments for well-known local conditions. Thus they are highly valued and respected by local people for their knowledge. Interestingly, the basic approach and understanding on which their medical knowledge rests has also been built upon to develop some of the most significant medical knowledge systems in the world— like those of Ayurveda, Unani and Siddha. But both these knowledge carriers and practitioners of medicine, that is 'ordinary women' and 'local healers', are despised by the practitioners of the codified medical knowledge systems, because their learning traditions are not from established texts.

On the other hand, the dominant medical knowledge of the past hundred years or so, that of scientific biomedicine, believes that most knowledge that makes claims to understanding the body and health are by and large irrelevant. So they are contemptuous of the entire frame of AYUSH treatments, whichever tradition they come from. Therefore, they believe that they ought to be substituted wherever possible. This is the perspective that has guided the making of health policy and public health structures in most parts of the country and the post-colonial period, with minor exceptions. So this is the structure of hierarchy between different medical knowledge systems, in which it becomes clear that the poor suffer the most—because the knowledge that they value is not respected and supported and the services that they deserve are not provided. It is in this context that women in panchayats can play a significant role.

There are three kinds of roles women can play—first, urge AYUSH departments that are based in their panchayats to provide the maximum service they are meant to; second, network with non-governmental organizations that have done significant work with strengthening local health traditions and extend the benefit of their work to their own panchayats. Both these will enable them to regain some confidence about the local health practices, specially those that are based on locally available herbs and materials, so that they are able to play the third and most important role, which is a long-term role in the health of their people.

Panchayats, Women and the Public Health System

In the public health system, the allocation and importance to the AYUSH systems has always been an insignificant part of the overall budget and planning, though there were always voices in the government that believed in the potential of these systems. From the primary health centre level upwards, every level of healthcare was meant to give people access to different systems of healing, so that they could choose whichever they felt would do them good. Given the skewed political economy of development processes however, overall healthcare, along with education suffered from lack of attention. So there has been an overall lack of doctors, para-medical personnel, medicines and other facilities, which was also the case with the AYUSH provisions. Wherever they existed, however, there were always two problems—they were viewed as the second-best option of treatment by both the doctors as well as patients. In this context, the value of AYUSH services could never be fully realized. Since the setting up of the National Rural Health

Mission, however, the provision of these services and facilities at least has become somewhat better. Under the Mission, in the Eleventh Plan the focus was on the idea of 'Mainstreaming AYUSH' which, according to the perspective of the government, was about getting practitioners and facilities of these systems to co-locate with allopathic systems at the lowest level upwards. This meant that people everywhere would, by and large, have the option of choosing whichever option of healthcare they preferred, when they visited a doctor with a complaint. This provision opens up several possibilities for healthcare for rural populations, but we will focus on two aspects to it. The first is that both doctors and patients need to have a positive attitude towards the AYUSH systems and believe that there are certain disease-conditions or complaints for which they could provide very effective treatment. This will ensure that patients begin to benefit from medical wisdom that reiterates the value of these systems world-wide, even after the last century of scepticism and doubt. The second is that these facilities are likely to become available only when local leadership knows what they are eligible for and constantly puts demands on the system to deliver. Undoubtedly leaders of panchayats would very well know this, having to negotiate for every little other provision for their constituents. With the new NRHM provisions, therefore, there is now an opportunity for panchayat leaders to push for certain healthcare institutions that are bound to be of long-term advantage for their people. The Twelfth Plan document, which is under preparation at the moment, is believed to envisage the next plan as a 'health-centred' document. It is expected to put even more provisions and possibilities in place, specially for the AYUSH sector and these should be carefully studied and taken advantage of.

Panchayats, Women and NGOs working on Local Health Traditions

The work of many non-governmental organizations in the area of health, particularly focused on Local Health Traditions has been consolidated over the last two decades or so. To take a few examples, these are the Foundation for the Revitalization of Local Health

Traditions (FRLHT), the Centre for Indian Knowledge Systems (CIKS) and the Rashtriya Guni Mission and Mira Sadgopal's movement for protecting the *dai* (as traditional birth attendants are known in many parts of India). They have emphasized that it is important to recognize that every area has Local Health Traditions and that they need to be accepted as legitimate medical knowledge, with all the due precautions. This has meant that these organizations have painstakingly identified local medical practitioners, folk healers and also local medicinal resources which have provided supportive healthcare, often in the absence of either state health services or private ones. The significance of this work is manifold. First, it has been able to identify medical knowledge that people in a region have always had, which is both effective and easily accessible. Often this knowledge is based on local flora, has been in use for a long time and the modes of usage have also been specified. Along with this, there are local medical practitioners, often illiterate and poor, like their patients, but known to have great knowledge of certain disease conditions and their remedies. So identifying LHTs has meant a discovery of people, nature and knowledge all at once. Often the sum of this knowledge, once put together, serves to indicate how much local health can be locally managed, which can be a great source of self-confidence for people that have been long neglected by both state and the market. A number of initiatives undertaken by these groups have been invaluable. They have helped document the knowledge of these practitioners in an attempt to show that they are comparable to those of any formally trained practitioner, whether of the biomedical or AYUSH tradition. They have also involved local people—men and women to collectively document the flora of the area, especially those with specifically known medicinal value to the local people or practitioners. This has helped people to recognize that many of these species of medicinal plants need to be actively protected or promoted through cultivation. So through the efforts of community or other collective organizations to conserve medicinal plant species that may be over harvested or becoming endangered, the concerns of people's health are sought to be tied into the health of the nature they are dependent on. Thus what seems like a focused problem-solving approach in terms of identifying local health traditions, can serve much larger purposes as well, because it ties in human interests with that of nature.

In this work, the experience of most organizations has been that women have taken an active part, sometimes even a lead in the organization and mobilization of these activities for health. They have become active partners with local healers in the battle for legitimacy of local health traditions, with the sole aim of ensuring the feasibility of the local health of people. The challenges faced here are the twin challenges of the legitimacy of the knowledge of healers, despite being outside the textual tradition and that of women, being outside the patriarchal division of knowledge—both significant markers of tradition that need to be opposed and fought effectively if we are to have more democratic spaces opening up in society, along with better healthcare provisions.

What is more, the work of these organizations that began with specific areas has spread to many states of the country, going on to show that none of these categories—of nature or knowledge—are exclusive to anyone area. Every part of the country, irrespective of the natural endowments, has a storehouse of medical knowledge waiting to be tapped into by people to become far more self-sufficient in terms of health. Wherever there is experience of once mobilizing and organizing people over these concerns, the lessons can be applied elsewhere, with consideration for the specificities of other places, experiences and traditions, of course. But this is one aspect of people's organization that can actually laterally spread its lessons across the country without too much difficulty. Women traditionally are accustomed to this kind of an exercise—within families, caste groups, communities—so the hope that they are able to apply those lessons to this very important aspect of their responsibility, is considerable. As stated at the outset, this has moved from being a personal to a political responsibility when women become leaders in panchayats.

Women, Panchayats and the Long-term Health of People

The aim of all initiation of women into public spaces ought to be, to my mind, two-fold. The first, that they learn new means and processes by which public life can be made better, which would orient them to working in new ways. At the same time, women are the repositories of traditional wisdom of many kinds, some of which could perhaps be profitably used for the greater common good. Like all such knowledge or wisdom, they ought to be valued, but also contested whenever necessary, something that traditional aspects of society do not often encourage. Women confined to personal spaces usually have both—knowledge/wisdom, but also the inhibition to express doubt or disagreement with what is passed down to them and believed to be sacrosanct. I believe that coming into public spaces ought to be able to help them in both—gain confidence in what they already know, as well as the ability to deal with any evidence that might show parts of it to need amendment. They ought to be able to make space for respecting both traditional and modern knowledge and the best place to start is the sphere of healthcare.

It is in all these respects that it should be possible to establish a fresh role for women with regard to AYUSH treatment. (Annexure II).

11

Improving Gross Domestic Healthcare Knowledge of Aam Aadmi

The Role of Women in Panchayats

Natasha Das

Introduction

The Government of India has launched the National Rural Health Mission, commonly called the NRHM with a goal to "*to improve the availability of and access to quality healthcare by people, especially for those residing in rural areas, the poor, women and children.*"[1] What is 'quality healthcare'? I know I am receiving 'quality healthcare' if the healthcare is right for my illness, if it is provided to me without any unnecessary delay, if it includes only those medical tests and procedures that I really need, if the healthcare does not cause me any harm, if it fits my needs and preferences and if it is not affected by such things as my gender, language, colour, age, place of residence or income. Unless I know what the right healthcare for my illness is or if I really need any of the medical tests and procedures advised, I will have no clue if I am being provided 'quality healthcare'. Only if a person has quality healthcare knowledge can he/she judge the availability and access of quality healthcare in their locality. This paper discusses how the women elected into the village panchayat can help improve the access to 'gross domestic healthcare knowledge' in their village.

Current Health Knowledge at the Grassroots

People in India have an outstanding knowledge of traditional medicine. A woman may not recall who told her that a paste of turmeric can heal a wound or that eating bottle gourd can increase the breast milk in a lactating woman. But she instinctively knows. However when it comes to modern medicine, the knowledge really is not enough. There is a need to provide healthcare knowledge that is accurate, effective and current.

Findings from the recent Tobacco Control Policy (TCP) India pilot survey suggest that the majority of smokers in India are not aware of the damage smoking causes to their health.[2] Even though there is an enormous volume of evidence of the harms caused by tobacco, most tobacco users worldwide are not fully aware of the damage it does to their bodies. Most people believe that the only damage it causes is lung cancer while tobacco actually harms nearly every organ of the body including the hair, the eyes, the oral cavity, the heart, the reproductive organs, the urinary bladder and even the toes.

A survey in four Western countries (USA, Canada, Australia and UK) conducted by the International Tobacco Control (ITC) project showed that 94 per cent of the responders believed that smoking causes lung cancer and 89 per cent believed smoking causes heart disease. In contrast, only 60 per cent of responders in India believed that smoking causes lung cancer and only 21 per cent responders in India believed that smoking causes heart disease.[2] Better knowledge about health effects of tobacco will lower the likelihood of initiation and improve the likelihood of quitting.

Here are a few true incidents that highlight the lack of attention people pay to their own health. The head master of a renowned school detected his diabetes only when there was bleeding in his eyes because of the side effects of diabetes. A young boy of a rich rural family lived with severe headache for four years and one day died suddenly due to bleeding in the brain. One of the arteries in his brain was deformed and could have been repaired if proper treatment was given. A boy from a doctor's family in a village had epileptic fits. He got every other form of non-medical treatment but no proper medical management. A cardiac surgeon in Delhi discovered that three arteries in his heart were blocked only after he had a heart attack. A health worker in a premier government hospital in a metropolitan city was misdiagnosed when the number of lumps kept increasing. An eminent Indian anaesthesiologist in UK was diagnosed with high blood pressure, when he fell down and his BP was measured at 200/160 in the ICU. This is just the tip of the iceberg for negligence towards health issues. Professional or non-professional, poor or rich, rural or urban, we all behave as '*Aam Aadmi*' when it comes to our own personal health.

Improved health knowledge enhances better health promoting behaviour in the community. The aim of quality health education/ knowledge is to develop among the people a sense of responsibility for their own health, for the health of the members of their family and the health of the community in which they live. This sense of responsibility imbibes in them a sense of confidence that their health is in their own hands, the confidence that they know how to prevent certain diseases, the confidence that they know what is wrong with their health, the confidence that they know what the available treatment modalities are and the confidence that they know when to see a healthcare professional.

Panchayat and Health

There is gross inadequacy in the funding for healthcare in India. The public expenditure on health systems is woefully low, just about 1 to 2 per cent of the total GDP. In a country of over a billion people this expenditure is also not evenly distributed. About 120 crore democratic Indian population cannot be allowed to fall sick and then their treatment aspects be addressed. We must stop as many menaces as possible at the grassroot level. People are discovering their diabetes, hypertension, cancer, etc., when it is already in a late stage with very unbearable level of discomfort or side effects. It is not true that such diseases can be detected only in the late stage.

They are detected at a late stage because people are unaware of the early signs and symptoms. Also because of high levels of privatization, and the commercial interests of pharmaceutical companies, it is often seen that many doctors themselves delay the treatment process or prescribe unnecessary or at times potentially harmful tests, procedures and medications.

With an aim to provide health services to even the remotest village, the government healthcare services in India are organized at different levels. The Primary Health Centre (PHC), at the core of rural health infrastructure in India, has both outpatient and outreach services. The outreach services are provided through sub-centres with the help of multipurpose health workers. Inpatient and more specialized services are provided at the Community Health Centre (CHC). Each sub-centre caters to a population of 5,000 people; each PHC to a population of 30,000 and each CHC to 100,000. Referral healthcare services are provided by district hospitals and medical college teaching hospitals.

Each village, however, does not have a sub-centre to provide healthcare service. But every village in India with a population of 500 or more has a gram panchayat. The gram panchayat is the village level institution for local self-governance under the Panchayati Raj structure. Health and sanitation are listed as one of the twenty-nine responsibilities of the Panchayati Raj institutions. The activities of the Panchayati Raj institutions include identification of the people in need of health services, monitoring the village level health workers, and primary and secondary healthcare facilities. The panchayats also play a pivotal role in planning, implementing and monitoring the interventions included under the NRHM. The NRHM guidelines state that the ASHA is responsible to the panchayat, i.e., the panchayat monitors the working of the ASHA. Though the Village Health, Sanitation and Nutrition Committee (VHSNC) is not directly answerable to the panchayat, the chief of the panchayat or the sarpanch is also a member of the committee and can adequately guide the committee from within.

It may be believed that the panchayat representatives do not take sufficient interest in the health problems of the village as they have twenty-eight other responsibilities to take care of. However, a study by the Institute of Social Sciences, New Delhi shows that elected women representatives in the panchayats help implementation of the Janani Surakshya Yojana in their locality and encourage pregnant women to have institutional child deliveries. Many women who are elected into the panchayat have an experience of having served as anganwadi workers or ASHAs. These women are expected to show more interest in the health issues concerning their village.

Gross Domestic Healthcare Knowledge: The Vision

As the panchayat already plays a role in providing and monitoring the health and sanitation, Swaasthya Sanchaar foresees a key role of the panchayat in disseminating health knowledge in their village.

Swaasthya Sanchaar, which literally means 'Health Communication' is a not-for-profit organization based in Delhi. Its main mission is to bring on-demand health knowledge in an easily consumable and accessible format within the reach of every individual in India.

Health Knowledge Dissemination through Print

Health knowledge is available in various forms. There are books, booklets, pamphlets, brochures, etc., obtainable in many different languages that bring health within the reach of people. Who buys those materials available in print, particularly, if it is about health and illness? Not many people buy a book on health issues. They may invest in a cine magazine, a fashion magazine or a magazine on fancy cars and watches, but very few households actually buy any books or magazines related to health unless some near and dear one suffers from a particular disease or there is an epidemic and one feels the urgent need to know about that particular epidemic disease.

Free magazines, books, etc. are also available on health. People pick up free brochures, from the doctor's clinic. Some free pamphlets on health issues appear with the day's newspaper. Many of these brochures and pamphlets are simply crumpled and discarded after a casual glance. Even when somebody reads a booklet or brochure on health, he/she may just stack it away after reading. And when the need arises to refer to something written in the book, the book may just have been misplaced and unavailable at that particular time. Even if the book is in hand, it often takes some time to go through the book to find the most relevant information needed at that hour. Also to be taken into consideration is the fact that around 40 per cent of Indians are illiterate and will not be able to read the information that is available in print form.

Health Knowledge Dissemination through Radio and Television

Extensive health information is also available in the audio and audiovisual format on radio and television. Television has been particularly successful in creating awareness about the polio vaccination programme.

Doordarshan which is managed by Prasar Bharati provides Information, Education and Communication (IEC) support to Health and Family Welfare. It telecasts health programmes during different time slots and such programmes reach out to people all across the country. Regional centres also telecast health shows and video spots in the regional languages.

Yet, neither radio nor television has emerged as a prominent medium for spread of healthcare knowledge. The drawback of radio and television in disseminating healthcare knowledge is that the programmes are hardly on demand. For example, a health show on television might have a health education programme today about eye infections and their treatment. But, you may be more interested in a programme on arthritis because of your chronic knee pain. Or they are broadcasting a show on radio this weekend about antenatal care of pregnant women and you have been waiting all week to hear this particular programme. What do you do if your mother-in-law insists on listening to the folk music on another radio channel instead, at that very time? Or you have unexpected guests at home and cannot switch on the radio in their presence? Can you go back to the programme later? Most probably, no!

Healthcare Knowledge on Demand

Swaasthya Sanchaar's vision of 'gross domestic healthcare knowledge' (GDHK) is to enhance the access to healthcare knowledge on demand. A person should be able to access health knowledge as and when he/she wants to and about the particular health issue that he or she needs. Also the healthcare knowledge should be available to the person not only in the language of the state he belongs to but in the very dialect that he speaks. For example, a person living in a village in Balasore district of Odisha should be able to access healthcare knowledge in Baleswari Odia and a person in a village in Sambalpur district should have access to healthcare knowledge in Sambalpuri Odia.

GDHK Hub

Swaasthya Sanchaar believes that an integrated approach is needed for availability of healthcare knowledge on demand, to improve the gross domestic healthcare knowledge at the grassroots.

The idea is to create in each village a GDHK hub. This will be a place where the most recent and accurate healthcare knowledge will be made available on demand to the people of the village. The panchayat can help identify an appropriate place in the village for such a hub.

Books, pamphlets, brochures, etc., need to be rewritten in the local dialect with ample and relevant illustrations for easy understanding and consumption. Multimedia kits such as CDs, DVDs, etc. will be made on common ailments. These CDs and DVDs will be in the local dialect. The hub will have provision for smaller viewing of such CDs and DVDs through a computer. Whenever people in the village want, provisions will be made for larger viewings with the help of a projector. As internet access continues to expand, it will serve as an important health resource. If the internet facility is made available at the GDHK hub, tele- or video-conferencing can be done with experts to discuss health issues. Regardless of their location, the internet will allow people to have access to a wide range of health information on a mouse click. However, there is a vast amount of false and potentially harmful information available on the internet. To avoid misconceptions, it is important to identify some websites that provide valid and accurate health information.

The panchayat will help identify key personnel in the village who can be trained about certain illnesses through contact programmes either in the same village or elsewhere. These trained health educators then become the medium for spread of the healthcare knowledge. Why identify such personnel from the same village? Because, they are the people in whom the villagers have utmost faith. These personnel can help spread GDHK through informal gatherings and discussions with the villagers. Such health educators can discuss health issues at a village fair, a temple, a rice field, or even during a baby shower. Villagers can also seek one-to-one consultations with them regarding specific health issues. The health educators of the village will be answerable to the panchayat.

Mobile phone technologies have demonstrated the incredible power of communication as an agent of social change. Spread of technology, affordability, increasing ease of use, increasingly large screen size and ever increasing number of various services, makes cell phones a potent tool to reach out to the masses, empower and connect them to the national growth in as many dimensions as possible. Swaasthya Sanchaar proposes the use of mobile phone technology in making timely, on-demand, and relevant health information available to people across all communities using pure voice as well as multimedia technology. When 3G services are available, multimedia content can be accessed over the telephony network with relative ease.

According to the UN study on sanitation, more Indians have access to a mobile phone than to a toilet.[3] Even households that do not have a radio or a television today have a mobile phone. Mobile phone text messaging (SMS) is being used to provide periodic health information. Education provided this way again may not be on demand.

We want to use mobile phone technology to provide health education on demand. The concept uses automated voicemail technology to answer the customer's queries. For example, a person will dial an assigned phone number for health education. Common diseases (5 to 10 common diseases from each specialty or sub-specialty of medical, paramedical and AYUSH domains) will be included in the database. As many as 70 dialects will be covered. Each village will be provided brochures listing the disease code for 450+ diseases and 70+ dialects. Anyone can dial the GDHK number (made available nationwide) and press the disease code and dialect code. They can then obtain audio information in an extremely lucid and relevant manner and can even talk to the doctor in their own dialect. The application is well-designed keeping the common Indian in mind.

Case Study: Breast Self-Examination

As a pilot project, we are working on spreading the knowledge about breast self-examination and empowering women across the country to help in early detection of breast cancer. We have successfully reached out to over 17,000 women across Delhi, Uttar Pradesh, Haryana, and Odisha and educated them about Breast Self-Examination (BSE). We use SMS services, various applications of telephone and IT to keep women in the loop for continuous motivation and support. It is now creating a spiralling effect in the community.

Breast self-examination is a method by which a woman can examine herself in the comforts of her own room and detect changes in the breast at the earliest. In India, when a woman visits a doctor, she may be asked if she has any problem in breathing, in digestion or even in her menstrual cycles. But, she is almost never asked about any problems in her breasts. It is always the woman herself who comes to the doctor with the complaint in her breast. So she needs to be alert in order to detect early changes. Sadly, only about 10-20 per cent of breast cancer cases in India are detected at an early stage. The majority are detected pretty late when the treatment options are fewer and much costlier. The main reason is ignorance. Most women do not know if they should see a doctor till it is quite late.

To increase awareness about breast self-examination (BSE), we conduct regular workshops where we teach women how to do a breast self-examination. We do this through slide presentations, oral discussions and mannequin demonstrations. Our presentations and discussions are in English, Hindi or any other regional language of

India depending on the profile of the attendees. Women are always asked to complete a short post-workshop written assignment. Some of the women are called forward to do a back demonstration on the mannequin. The rest of the attendees are asked to point out if there are any errors or if some information is missing when the back demonstration is done. Various incentives are provided for better acceptance of the programme and actual empowerment of the participants. All attendees are provided certificates for their attendance. These women are then encouraged to spread the knowledge to at least one small group of ladies and identify key persons who can spread the knowledge further. Nurses, ASHAs and anganwadi workers who attend our programmes are encouraged to teach this technique to all the women in their villages.

What is really encouraging about these workshops which we conduct is that there is never a limit to the number of ladies we speak to at one go. One of our workshops had just seven women at a private gathering in Bhubaneswar. Another workshop had over 600 women in the Special Protection Group (SPG) campus in Dwarka, Delhi. We speak about BSE on demand and if there is a group of even three ladies who wish to learn BSE, we are prepared to teach them the steps. We send SMS, email, and make phone calls (depending on need and feasibility) to our participants to practise BSE regularly, spread the knowledge and extend any other kind of health-based help. Though we understand that an all ladies gathering may be the most comfortable to some, we also speak at combined gatherings of men and women. It is important that the group is comfortable enough to let it be a two-way interactive discussion. Our experience over the years shows that a simple lecture on BSE or a video presentation is not as effective as an open two-way communication where we also answer any queries and clear any myths about the breast, breast self-examination and breast cancer.

Information is also made available as slide presentations with voice recordings that can be shared through email exchange. We have the material ready in English, Hindi, Odia, Punjabi, Kannada, etc., and are working at preparing materials in other languages as well.

For making the information about breast cancer available on demand through mobile phone technology, we have a working prototype in place, where 30 callers can call simultaneously. The system allows the caller to talk to a doctor. We are adding complete information on HIV/AIDS and diabetes to this service. This information is currently available in Hindi and English. We have the script ready in other languages too and are working at making these available through a phone call so that health education is available literally, at the person's fingertips.

Conclusion

Quality health education is needed to empower people to make right decisions about their own health and the health of those close to them. There is extensive health-related information available in the print media, radio and television. However, there is hardly any health information available to individuals on demand that people can access as and when they want to at their own convenience.

Gross domestic healthcare knowledge base is a concept where we want to make health information available to each individual at his or her domestic residence or at least within reach in the village or locality where they reside. They can also talk to a doctor in their own dialect. This health information will be available on demand whenever and wherever the individual wants to access it. Providing such information to each village is possible only with the cooperation of the respective panchayat members.

REFERENCES

1. India Go: National Rural Health Mission (2005-2012): Mission Document. Edited by Welfare MoHaF; 2005-2012.
2. Sansone, G.C.; Raute, L.J.; Fong, G.T.; Pednekar, M.S.; Quah, A.C.; Bansal-Travers, M.; Gupta, P.C.; Sinha, D.N.: Knowledge of Health Effects and Intentions to Quit among Smokers in India: Findings from the Tobacco Control Policy (TCP) India Pilot Survey. *Int J Environ Res Public Health* 2012, 9(2): 564-578.
3. India has more mobile phones than toilets: UN report [http://www.telegraph.co.uk/news/worldnews/asia/india/7593567/India-has-more-mobile-phones-than-toilets-UN-report.html]

12

Keeping Good Health where there are No Doctors

Alternative System of Treatment

Saurabh Gahlote

Dr. Saurabh Gahlote in his interactions with the elected women representatives asked what we understand by health? Is it weight, physical dimension or the colour? He said that none of these definitions are correct. Health is when an individual is disease-free physically and mentally. Physically we should not have any kind of communicable or non-communicable diseases. All the vital parameters of an individual should be within normal range. He observed that communicable diseases are transmitted from one individual to another, the mode of transmission may be different with different diseases.

Further he emphasized issues of sanitation and cleanliness in ensuring women's well-being. According to him, sanitation plays a very important role especially in villages where at times closed toilets are not available and people go to open fields. If the villages are kept clean "then all of you will not need me, i.e., 'a doctor'". He added that "you should not only look after your families' health but also your villagers' health as these villages make a city and cities make a state and these states make the country, so if our village is healthy our country will also be healthy". He also called all the elected representatives the "prime ministers" of their respective villages, and it becomes the responsibility of these prime ministers to take the village and villagers in the right direction.

How to Treat the Seasonal Common Diseases with Home Remedies

Dr. Gahlote pointed out that in case of loose motions and/or vomiting, try and give clean liquids to the patient as it may give some hydration to him/her and may act as a life-saving device. Even if the patient keeps vomiting or having continuous loose motions he/she should be kept on clean liquids otherwise, the patient gets dehydrated and the situation may cause a serious impact on his/her life. Try and add a small pinch of salt and sugar to the clean water and this will act as (ORS) solution. Anyone can check if the patient is dehydrated. For that one needs to pinch the skin of the abdominal area. After pinching if the skin retains its original shape without any wrinkles then it can be surmised that the patient is not dehydrated. However, if it is not the case, then one needs to work on the hydration part initially. Try and avoid milk and its products during loose motions and vomiting as this may cause further infection.

There is another misconception in our society that if anybody has fever, s/he should be fully covered with blankets and this will make him better. However, the fact is if somebody has fever s/he should be fully exposed and should be in the bare minimum of clothes so that temperature transfer can take place and body temperature abates. High temperature may cause seizures which may be fatal for life. Another misconception is that if during fever cold sponging is done with ice cold or cold water then it may cause pneumonia, which may happen for other reasons and not only this.

He advised all the elected members to eat only fresh and less oily food. Being the caretaker of the house, it is the responsibility of the woman of the household to ensure that she is not over cooking the vegetables. They should avoid consuming stale food as it is a good source of infection and specially in summer when bacteria grow really fast in food and fruits. There is a great possibility that the RO facility may not be available in villages or in some houses but one can boil and cool the water to make it bacteria free for oral consumption.

Speaking on the diseases of winter he said, asthma and heart disease are some of the most common ailments found in our country. Diabetes is becoming very common nowadays. He further added that a person who has diabetes may not get a cardiac pain as in diabetes, the sensation of getting pain is reduced and hence it is a painless attack. He advised that in winter if one notices any elderly or diabetic patient with severe breathing difficulty, sweating, and giddiness, then s/he should be given medical help ASAP. If there is no other remedy that may help then medical assistance is a must to save one's life.

Pneumonia is another disease which has become more common because of the low temperature, particularly in winter. Elderly people should be advised to cover the upper part of the body since that part is more prone to respiratory infections. If possible, get all the elderly people vaccinated for pneumonia. Thyroid is another disease on which Dr. Gahlote shed light. He observed that although not seasonal, it is very important for all of us. A special mention may be made regarding its impact on women since it leads to infertility. Talking about thyroid, he observed that if anyone has sudden hair fall, any recent change of voice or any sudden weight gain, then it may be due to that dreaded disease.

Commenting on the incidence of diseases in the monsoon, he mentioned that the rainy season is the worst in terms of disease spread. He felt that many female representatives come from the place where there is abundant rain and in such places one should ensure that they reheat the food before every consumption. In the rainy season there is high possibility of rain water getting clogged which acts as the breeding ground for different kinds of mosquitoes which may cause diseases like dengue. In the past some parts of northern India have encountered many deaths owing to dengue. So we should ensure that there is proper drainage of water in our respective villages.

He maintained that no disease is small, even the smallest disease may have serious consequences. He added that not only is cleanliness and prevention necessary, what is also very important is that all of us should have a healthy and balanced diet. He requested all the women present at the meeting not to treat themselves as second class citizens in one's own family. Each one of them should give equal importance in terms of quality and quantity of food, as the women are the most prominent members in the family. One should remember that because of women the whole family remains healthy. He also acknowledged that the real wealth of the family are the women and how can they be considered less important?

Finally, he added that although it is all about care without a doctor but during pregnancy one must not miss a visit to a doctor. It is very important for a woman, and for the health of the baby to visit the doctor regularly and get the delivery done by him or a trained *dai*. Last but not the least, he observed that on the issue of female foeticide, we should all stand together and stop it. The most significant role can be played by the elected representatives because at some point of time all of us have been in our mother's womb and had she not given birth to us, we would not have been listening to the speech.

13

Panchayats, Women and Health for All*

Nupur Tiwari

India has seen unprecedented economic growth over the last decade, but maternal mortality and morbidity continue to be unacceptably high. More than 1 lakh mothers in the country die each year as a result of pregnancy-related causes (UNICEF, n.d.). One study reports that for each maternal death, 15-20 mothers suffer from serious childbirth-related health impairments (Datta *et al.*, 1980).

Child morbidity and mortality is also very high in India. The major causes of child death are lack of safe drinking water and proper sanitation as well as poor hygiene. In the developing countries around 90 per cent of all avoidable mortality in almost all age/sex groups is from communicable diseases, most notably malaria, TB, cholera, and to a lesser extent HIV/AIDS (Mills and Shillcut, 2004). A great portion of the Indian rural population lack basic sanitation and safe drinking water.

What makes the situation more disturbing is that most maternal deaths are avoidable (Bhatia, 1993; UNFPA, 2002). Poor maternal health outcomes and pregnancy-related care are rooted in structural factors such as poverty and illiteracy, as well as other factors including lack of awareness of appropriate health practices and prompt decision-making. The resources available in the rural areas for

---

* Chairperson's Remarks.

healthcare are meagre, particularly Reproductive and Child Health (RCH). A majority of women indicated that there are severe constraints in access to government maternal health services.

The 73rd Constitutional Amendment makes it mandatory that functions related to the provision of primary healthcare-maternal health and family welfare are the responsibility of the PRIs. Besides, the various development sector departments come under the functional jurisdiction of the district panchayat.

Creating a health system with the panchayats being made responsible for supervising and monitoring health services seems an ideal model.

The health department staff (including the doctors and para-medical staff at the PHC) do not consider themselves answerable to panchayats. From the viewpoint of health professionals the elected representatives are not technically qualified to assess their work. The point which is often missed is that it is not technical expertise of the elected representatives, but it is their role in identifying the needs and inadequacies in healthcare delivery and supervising the attendance of health functionaries. To make people aware and to increase the acceptance of the facilities provided under health and family welfare programmes, one of the important efforts is the involvement of panchayat elected representatives for implementation of the programmes, as these people generally command great confidence and respect from the community.

Panchayat members are responsible for carrying out the following:

- Creating awareness among the local people about the main aspects of public health and helping in different aspects of curative and preventive care.
- Overseeing and helping in implementing the schemes of maternal child healthcare facilities.
- Controlling infectious diseases such as diarrhoea, malaria, HIV-AIDS, and other diseases and conditions such as leprosy, blindness, etc.
- Maintaining the birth-death register.
- Creating awareness among people about small family norms

and identifying whether the means for family planning are available to every eligible couple of their locality.

- Overseeing the nutrition level of local and school children including the ICDS (Integrated Child Development Scheme) programme and mid-day meals.

The involvement of panchayat members is required in improving the healthcare facilities in rural areas. They (panchayat) can take initiatives for the improvement of the public health system through initiatives to improve safe drinking water and sanitation.

The panchayat members can assist in campaigning for the immunization programme, maternal child health programmes, public health and sanitation, work for communicable diseases, and in registration of births and deaths. In the child immunization efforts, specifically the pulse polio programme, was given top priority among other activities,

Panchayats have a crucial role to make gender planning of health realistic. It is important that local women are accompanied (and not led) by health planners, social scientists and others; they receive timely and appropriate information and skills, and they make decisions leading to gender health and family welfare.

14

Women in Panchayats are the Practical Guide to Health Issues*

Suraj Kumar

I welcome you all. Today if someone casts doubts regarding your knowledge in matters of health nobody would believe him or her. You are aware of the health issues and it is for you to find solutions. I know that in 1978 in Alma-Ata, Kazakhstan, almost all the countries of the world had taken a pledge to achieve the aim of 'health for all' in the ten years that were to follow. Keeping in mind the fact that all the resources are available to us and if they are to be used properly, it is not impossible for us to achieve the goal of 'health for all'. (Annexure III)

The second pledge was made in India on April 24, 1993. This day is also observed as the Panchayat day and the pledge made then was regarding the participation of women and the strengthening of the panchayats. There have been several achievements in these areas and a remarkable fall in the infant mortality rate. As far as the Panchayati Raj system is concerned, no one can now say that it is not a part of India's political system. Probably it is also rare now to hear that the panchayats are weak bodies and hence should not be given rights. Such an observation was probably made in the past but the panchayat now has become a political institution. To ensure your rights in the panchayats is a commitment and a pledge.

---

* Women delegates were greeted during the celebrations.

The role of panchayats in fulfilling both these promises is considerable. I recall an incident during the rule of Sri Digvijay Singh, the management of the health department was given over to the panchayats and as a result the doctors went on strike. Issues like what understanding do panchayats have and how would things be done were also discussed. Owing to the protest, a number of progressive-looking steps had to be called off. Today if someone were to say that you who are a part of the panchayats have no awareness of health issues, it is unlikely that he or she will be taken seriously. This is a pointer to the fact that there has been considerable progress in the thought and attitudes. Now we have the opportunity to think about how to implement the ideas into action. This is because people today can no longer wait for the expert in order to have access to better health. They need an immediate solution to this problem. So in the coming three days of the seminar, we should raise our voice about what should the panchayats and women do for the mission 'health for all'. For this, intellectual conversation should take place and along with that practical solutions and practical issues should be raised as to how it should be done. I congratulate Smt. Shraddhaji who made an important suggestion in this regard. I wish that it would be an ideal situation if you were seated with the speaker and the few experts and you should say what you want and how things can be done. Finally, I am happy that cancer specialists, heart specialists and political analysts are participating in this seminar.

> "Only that man can be said to be really healthy who has a sound mind in a sound body. The relation between the body and the mind is so intimate that if either of them goes out of order the whole system would suffer."
>
> —Mahatma Gandhi
>
> —Key to Health, 1942-44

15
Voices from the Field

A : *National Rural Health Mission and Sex Selective Abortion**

Through the 73rd Constitutional Amendment, Panchayati Raj Institutions were provided with 33 per cent reservation for women which have a significant and positive impact on the gender relations in society as well as on the position of women. The women PRI members have most of the time taken an active role in polio eradication, health camps and mobilizing women for health services. The National Rural Health Mission (NRHM)was launched in 2005 to bring about a holistic and multi-pronged strategy to improve the outreach of healthcare in rural India. The importance of the role of PRIs in operationalization of NRHM cannot be underscored. There are three main reasons for the criticality of the PRIs for the NRHM. Firstly, intersectoral convergence and community ownership. Secondly, the Accredited Social Health Activist (ASHA) to strengthen village level delivery. Thirdly, the Village Health,

---

*States Represented : Jammu & Kashmir, Uttarakhand, Himachal Pradesh, Punjab, Haryana, Uttar Pradesh, Rajasthan.

Chair : Bijaylaxmi Nanda is a Senior Lecturer, Miranda House, Delhi University.

Rapporteur : Ghanashyama Kushwaha is a Ph.D. Scholar, Delhi University.

Sanitation and Nutrition Committee (VHSNC) to form links between the gram panchayat and the community, to ensure that the health plan is in harmony with the overall plan. Census 2011 produced the worst picture of declining child sex ratio in India. There is a strong trend of daughter aversion in society and misuse of medical technology to bring about sex-selective abortion and sex selection. While the NRHM guidelines give a secondary role to the PRIs in health and family welfare issues, prevention of sex selection is not clearly articulated in the guidelines. But where there is a political will and involvement of right-based NGOs the issue gets highlighted and there is a visible involvement of all stakeholders on the issue. In Haryana, Himachal Pradesh and Kashmir this involvement has led to a sensitization of community members. However, in most other states the issue is not given the attention it deserves. Dowry is one of the main reasons for killing the girl child but not the sole one. This has to be understood by women in the context of gender relations.

Parveena Rizvi, a member of the self-help group from Jammu & Kashmir, observed that the village health committee meeting is held once a month and the issues on the prevention of sex-selective abortions are discussed. She also expressed concern about certain clauses of the Pre-conception and Pre-natal Diagnostic Techniques (PCPNDT) Act, particularly monitoring through the tracking of pregnancy. In doing so, the women feel very harassed. She added that "In Jammu and Kashmir, ASHA maintains a diary where she records the number of babies born and are expected to be born on different dates and plays a significant role in making women aware of their health". In the process, she tries to find out about the cases of sex-selective abortions.

Asha Devi, a sarpanch from Jaipur, Rajasthan, emphasized the question of making women aware of the PCPNDT Act. She is also an active social activist and looks after the proper utilization of funds. Regarding the amount of money coming to the village health committee she pointed out that about Rs.10,000 is given to the village health committee by the government under NRHM. She said, "The government should issue licenses to the hospitals for keeping ultrasound machines and hospitals must keep records of doing the same". She suggested that "our society is a male dominated society and hence there is discrimination against the girl child". "*Is anyay ke khilaaf hum sabhi mahilaaon ko milkar sangharsh karna chahiye*" (all women should fight together against this injustice).

Some other participants like Kalpana, sarpanch from Hissar, Haryana, said that she did not have any knowledge about the Village Health Committee. She also said, "*hume NRHM ke bare mei koyi jankari nahi hai*" (we do not have any knowledge about NRHM). Most of the women participants from Madhya Pradesh expressed the same view.

However, Smita Devi another sarpanch from Hissar, Haryana said that she with other women in the village go collectively to other villages to mobilize women and persuade them not to abort the foetus of a girl child, and urge the use of toilets, etc. She said, "*Hum shouchalaya ke nirman gharon mei aur ladki ke janma lene par uska panjikaran karane par jyada jor dete hain*" (we emphasize the construction of toilets inside the houses and registration of girls being born).

Another NGO activist told a true story about Sumitra Devi from Haryana that even after having two girl children, the third time she did not opt for abortion even though her mother-in-law compelled her to go in for abortion. Another woman, Munni Devi from Jhajhjhar (Haryana) an anganwadi worker, said that "women need to understand their role and duty towards the society as a whole and prevent girls from being aborted". She said, "*ladkiyan aaj ladkon se kam nahi hain, aaj hamari rashtrapati bhi to aurat hai, hume unhe padhana chahiya*" (girls are not less than boys today, even our president is a lady, we need to educate them).

A sarpanch from Madhya Pradesh affirmed that there is an *abhiyan* (campaign) called "*Beti Bachao*" for which the slogan is "*beti hai to kal hai*". Another *abhiyan* called "*Mitaani*" which means "the best friend" operated in Madhya Pradesh and Chhattisgarh to save the girl child on a large scale.

Sarita, a sarpanch from Ghazipur, Uttar Pradesh mentioned that there is no Village Health Committee/ Rogi Kalyan Committee in her panchayat. She said, "*paisa kab aata hai aur kahan chala jata hai pata nahi chalta*" (when money comes and where it is spent we do not know.

Lalmani, another sarpanch from Ghazipur, said, "*dusre aadmi sahyog nahi karte aur meeting ke bare mein nahi batate aur apne hi kar lete hain*" (other male panchayat members do not cooperate with her and they do not let her know about the meetings. They conduct the meeting all by themselves). She did not know about the PCPNDT Act but she was aware that girl child abortion is considered to be a crime. She said that women members do not participate in panchayat meetings and their respective husbands do all the official work. She observed that women should grab their power and rights, since nobody would be willing to part with it.

Another active woman representative from Gorakhpur, Teeja Devi said that she has taken strong action against alcoholism, and sex determination to prevent girl child abortion. She is engaged in practising organic agriculture and imparts training to other women to use organic manure. She works with ASHA to look after pregnant women in her village panchayat. She said, "*hum akele jaakar kaam karate hain aur nahi karne par aur mahilaaon ko lekar dharne par baith jaate hain*" (she herself goes to get work done and if work is not done she along with other women go on for strike). She added, "*samaj tabhi vikas karega jab aurat shashakta hogi*" (society can develop only when women are empowered).

Reshma, a sarpanch from Maharajganj, Uttar Pradesh, maintained that her agricultural land was taken away by the upper caste people illegally. She is illiterate yet she realizes the importance of education and emphasized that women need to be educated so that nobody could exploit them. She said, "*ab hum samajh gaye hain ki hum sab kuch kar sakte hain, hum kisi se kam nahi hain*" (now we have got to know that we can do everything, we are not less than anyone).

This is clear from the above discussion that women are now more assertive for their rights given in the Constitution after the 73rd Constitutional Amendment Act in 1993. But there is a dire need to educate them and make them aware of health issues. To obtain the objectives under NRHM, enlisting of NGOs to build capacities of PRIs so that they are sensitized about gender issues and awareness can go a long way in curbing sex selection. Within the existing programmes and mechanism, the ASHAs and ANMs can be used in various ways including consciousness raising, facilitating and monitoring processes to create an enabling environment for the survival of girl children. Partnerships with NGOs, medical professionals and other service providers under the aegis of the NRHM on the issue of sex selection will be able to deliver the desired result at the practical level. At last we can say that through a capacity building process of elected women representatives and by working with gender sensitive NGOs, the phenomenon of sex selection can be countered. And thereby gender equality and health for all can be achieved in rural India by NRHM.

B: *Health Insurance and Women—Role of Panchayati Raj Institutions.**

Panchayati Raj Institutions (PRIs) of India has been entrusted with 29 subjects by the Eleventh Schedule of the Constitution of India after the 73rd Amendment in 1993 for the economic and social development and improving the quality of people's lives. Accordingly, health in its broad sense is an important function of PRIs.

Thus in this perspective, the National Rural Health Mission was launched in 2005 by the Government of India with a goal of availability of and access to quality healthcare services. It aims at infrastructural development in the basic healthcare delivery system and caring determinants of good health such as nutrition, sanitation, hygiene and safe drinking water. It also targets: (i) mainstreaming the Indian systems of medicine to facilitate healthcare, (ii) reducing regional imbalance in health infrastructure, (iii) pooling resources, (iv) integration of organizational structures, optimization of health

---

**States Represented* : Arunachal Pradesh, Himachal Pradesh, Odisha, Tamil Nadu, and West Bengal.

Chair : Smt. Suparna Ganguly, Sr. Faculty and Convener of State Support Centre (PMEYSA), SIPRD, Kalyani, West Bengal.

manpower, (v) decentralization and district management of health programmes, (vi) community participation and ownership of assets, (vii) induction of management and financial personnel into the district health system, and (viii) operationalizing community health centres into functional hospitals meeting Indian Public Health Standards in each block of the country.

Thus NRHM started its work in 18 states (which are weak in Public Health Indicators and have inadequate health infrastructure) with the following components:

- Introducing Accredited Social Health Activists (ASHAs)
- Strengthening sub-centres.
- Strengthening Primary Health Centres (PHC).
- Strengthening Community Health Centres (CHC).
- District Health Plan amalgamating the grassroot level health plan.
- Converging Sanitation and Hygiene.
- Strengthening Disease Control Programme.
- Public-Private Partnership for Public Health (PPP).
- New Health Financing Mechanisms.
- Reorienting Health Education.

The ninth component was New Health Financing Mechanisms under which Rashtriya Swasthya Bima Yojana or (RSBY) started rolling from April 1, 2008. It aims at providing health insurance coverage for Below Poverty Line (BPL) families. Beneficiaries under RSBY are entitled to hospitalization coverage up to ₹ 30,000 for most of the diseases that require hospitalization. The government has even fixed the package rates for the hospitals for a large number of interventions.

Objectives of the Discussion

Under this perspective the main objective of the group discussion is to know the status of health insurance in various states and the role of panchayats. To fulfil the objectives the enabling objectives are:

(a) To find out the condition of health of women.
(b) To list the services provided under NRHM .
(c) To know whether there is any state initiative regarding health other than NRHM.
(d) To find out the state of health insurance.
(e) To find out the role of panchayats.
(f) To find the gaps (if any) in healthcare delivery services.
(g) To find some policy implications to overcome the crisis.

Findings

- According to Elected Women Representatives (EWRs) of Himachal Pradesh.
- They don't have any information either about NRHM or about Health Insurance under RSBY.
- However, they are aware about the provision of maternity benefit scheme, Janani Suraksha Yojana, (JSY) which is an important component of the NRHM.
- Thus women in general do not get any facilities of NRHM as they lack information on NRHM.
- But EWRs have information about the State's Scheme, Jachha Bachha Janani Suraksha Yojana (JBJSY) which provides various facilities like:
  (i) Free Medicine ,
  (ii) Institutional Delivery,
  (iii) Immunization, and
  (iv) Nutritional Diet, etc.

On the other hand, the EWRs of Himachal Pradesh don't know who will provide these facilities or where to go or how these facilities can be obtained by the women.

- Thus the general health status of women has not improved.
- But no RSBY is available in Himachal Pradesh. There is insufficient information regarding healthcare delivery services or health insurance services.
- Another problem, raised by the EWRs that though they

have been elected in 2011, but they do not have any training either about panchayats nor about health.

- However, a service of free ambulance under Atal Behari Rashtriya Yojana is running in Himachal Pradesh.

It has been found from the group discussion with the EWRs of Arunachal Pradesh that all the services under NRHM run in Arunachal Pradesh like:

- ASHA, institutional delivery, immunization, health infrastructure development, etc: But the services are not so easily available and transparent.
- EWRs have insufficient information regarding services or service providers or about the funding of NRHM.
- Thus they cannot play the role towards the people effectively.
- EWRs also suffer from filtered information or from the non-cooperation of the officials of the health department.
- They face the lack of coordination of various departments.
- But according to EWRs, Integrated Child Development Services (ICDS) or Total Sanitation Campaigns (TSC) run well in the state though the provisions of Janani Suraksha Yojana are not available there.

Experience of EWRs from Tamil Nadu is pathetic. According to them:

- The panchayat system is not at all honoured as local self-government.
  Administration is more powerful than the panchayat system.
- Panchayat election has taken place recently, i.e., in 2012. But training has not been done.
- Political intervention from the top is so acute that the EWRs cannot work.
- EWRs do not know about the schemes, especially they do not have any information regarding NRHM or the Health Insurance.

It has been found from the group discussion with the EWRs of Assam that :

- EWRs are only aware about the MGNREGS and IGNOAPS.
- Health scenario is so distressful. There is shortage of medicine as well as that of conveyance at the grassroot level.
- There is no rural dispensary. There is only a district hospital which is at a distance from the poor.

EWRs of West Bengal expressed their views that:

- Services under NRHM available at grassroots are—
  - (i) Vaccination,
  - (ii) Institutional Delivery,
  - (iii) ASHA,
  - (iv) Health Insurance,
  - (v) Development of health infrastructures, and
  - (vi) Services of health functionaries.
- At the grassroots level Integrated Child Development Service (ICDS) plays an important role in the development of women and children.
- State's own initiative, Community Health Care Management Initiative (CHCMI) plays a role towards the development of Children and Women. Under CHCMI, gram panchayats act as the nodal agency to organize regular fourth Saturday meetings with functionaries of health and ICDS for monitoring on public health indicators and to give assistance to the Gram Unnayan Samiti (GUS) and SHG for better implementation of this programme. Gram Unnayan Samiti (GUS) is the arm of gram panchayats which undertake different activities to improve public health indicators in consultation with the above functionaries and to help selected SHG so that the SHG can undertake monitoring at the community level. There are also Functional Committee of Public Health (FC) of

GUS which undertakes activities of public health on behalf of the GUS. In this initiative Self Help Groups work as the agents of change to conduct a base line survey and to monitor three basic public health indicators, viz., anti-natal care of pregnant women, immunization of children (0-1 year) and weighing of babies (0-3 years).

- Total Sanitation Campaign is also another scheme.
- Rogi Kalyan Samiti is actively participating and monitoring the health schemes and health infrastructures.
- Self Help Groups are strong workers towards fulfilling the parameters of NRHM.

Rashtriya Swasthya Bima Yojana runs well. Unorganized sector workers belonging to the BPL category and their family members (a family unit of five) are the beneficiaries under the scheme. Implementing agencies will verify the eligibility of the unorganized sector workers and their family members who are proposed to be benefited under the scheme. The beneficiaries will be issued smart cards for the purpose of identification. The beneficiary is eligible for such in-patient health care insurance benefits designed by the state governments based on the requirements of the people/ geographical area. The following minimum benefits are available in the package/scheme:

- The unorganized sector worker and his family (unit of five) will be covered.
- The total sum insured will be ₹ 30,000 per family per annum on a family floater basis.
- Cashless attendance to all covered ailments.
- Hospitalization expenses, taking care of most common illnesses with as few exclusions as possible.
- All pre-existing diseases to be covered.
- Transportation costs (actual with maximum limit of ₹ 100 per visit) within an overall limit of ₹ 1,000.
- But there are some complaints against the RSBY scheme, such as, (i) beneficiaries are not informed about the procedure of how to obtain the benefits; (ii) most of the

enlisted nursing homes/private hospitals are very reluctant to provide the services and they refer the case to somewhere else, and (iii) the enlisted nursing homes/private hospitals give false bills.

Policy Implications/Suggestions

After the discussion the following suggestions have emerged from the groups:

(1) There must be rigorous training for Elected Representatives about the available governmental schemes (both central and state).

(2) Flow of information should exist. Information should be disseminated through EWRs, Mahila Mandals (Self-Help Groups), village level mother's committee and Bharat Nirman Swechha Sebak (recently grown through Lab to Land initiative of the central government).

(3) There must be vertical and horizontal coordination between Elected Representatives and officials of line departments so that the communication gaps can be mended and developmental works can be accelerated.

(4) There must be a clear cut Activity Mapping at each state so that the functionaries at various levels can understand their duties, responsibilities and limitations. And accordingly they can perform effectively and implement various schemes efficiently.

(5) Undermining the local self-government dominance of officials has made the situation grave in so many states. Thus fund, function and functionary should be devolved effectively to PRIs for the sake of people and panchayati raj.

(6) The sarpanch-pati system or the male intervention should be abolished.

(7) Health is a pro-woman parameter. Thus women representatives can do well in this sector rather than males. EWRs should be trained very well about health and allied

subjects and about their responsibilities. And they should be taught how to communicate with the people.

(8) EWRs must monitor the enlisted hospitals and nursing homes under RSBY so that service delivery can be checked.

(9) EWRs should have close contacts with the people so that they can perform effectively and people can be benefited optimally.

(10) Gender responsive health budget should be introduced in the Planning process so that the various health demands (locality-based) and requirements can be fulfilled.

(11) Own resource generation by panchayats should be encouraged so that more demands on health and others can be fulfilled.

(12) Health Card should be introduced for each household at grassroots level so that the target-based (children, aged people, adolescent girls, pregnant mothers, addicted youths, AIDS patients, TB patients, leprosy patients, etc.) health status can be monitored and accordingly necessary arrangements can be done.

(13) There must be an Association of Elected Women Representatives at GP level, block level, district level, state level and also at national level so that the real crisis or demand can be addressed and the charter of demand can be acknowledged in national or sub-national policy implications.

(14) The system of compulsory exposure visits across the states and districts should be introduced so that exchange of opinions and ideas can take place and elected representatives can be motivated towards the ultimate goal.

C : *Government Health Policies and Women*★

Women's health continues to be a neglected area with very little attention for mother and child health services. Women and young girls face appalling health conditions and impediments owing to inadequate healthcare resources and financial protection. To address regional health problems and issues, more than 50 elected women representatives came together from Karnataka, Himachal Pradesh, Madhya Pradesh and Bihar. Discussions in this group focused on the extent of availability of health facilities, medical health insurance schemes and health resource policy initiatives taken up by the government. Some of their experiences were shared and women sought regular assistance from the government for the upliftment of the poor health status of women.

To increase the proportion of institutional deliveries, an innovative government scheme, i.e., Janani Suraksha Yojana (JSY), exists in the states of Madhya Pradesh and Himachal Pradesh in which cash assistance is given to pregnant women for institutional delivery (@₹ 700) and a little less (@₹ 500) for home delivery. But during emergencies women felt that they are unable to avail of the facilities as they have to travel a long distance (40 kms) to reach a health centre which is unaffordable for them. Despite the existence of JSY, which is confined only for Scheduled Castes in the State of Himachal Pradesh, there is no proper streamlining of health workers' duties. For instance, ASHA's duties is given to an anganwadi worker and the latter is unable to do justice to the given task. Existence of corruption is evident in issuing the birth certificates for newborn babies as they are not given at once even after payment (₹ 1000 or ₹ 2000) to the health worker/pradhan. Women from Kolar and Hassan districts of Karnataka mentioned that despite the existence of annual cash incentives of ₹ 10,000 for ASHA for monitoring and accompanying pregnant women, the amount is not released at times as there is no flexibility in the government's approach towards workers and in many places vacant posts remain unfilled. In Jhabhua district of Madhya Pradesh, the usage of both ayurvedic and allopathic medicines was reported by a few women.

States : Karnataka, Bihar, Himachal Pradesh and Madhya Pradesh.

Chair : Tulsi Patel, Professor of Sociology, Delhi School of Economics, Delhi University.

Rapporteur : S. Syamala, Research Officer, Institute of Social Sciences, New Delhi.

Nevertheless, in Karnataka for the care of a girl child across the life cycle amongst poverty-affected families, an amount (₹ 10,000) is deposited by the government (Bhagyalakshmi deposit scheme) after birth which becomes 1 lakh after 18 years. Even in Muzaffarpur district, Bihar, a special caretaker scheme for malnourished newborn babies is implemented wherein ₹ 750 is being given per day for 21 days to the families who have such babies. Though the initiatives were taken by the government, there is a need for adequate cash transfer from the government to the gram panchayats. Another problem is the insufficient remuneration given by the panchayats for the women members working in the rural areas so out of compulsion from men of the households they were forced to work for MGNREGA but the job cards are not handed to women by the agents. Therefore, in Muzaffarpur, Bihar, women said that they desperately need financial protection due to the absence of a relevant health policy and many of them are unaware of the existence of the government medical insurance scheme despite the presence of self-help groups. Only in the state of Karnataka, the government agricultural cooperative society has an insurance scheme which provides ₹ 250 per head for one year for BPL families. In addition, a welfare committee has been developed by the health centre commission to generate and use funds.

A few suggestions given by the representatives were under the JSY scheme corrupt-free disbursement of cash transfers for pregnant women, regularization of incentives and payment for ASHAs without undue delay, development of affordable technologies like scan machines, launching of public medical insurance schemes targeting poor families for financial protection, trying to create awareness amongst women about the benefits of national medical insurance schemes not only for reproductive health services but also for other ailments and enhancement of health resources, On the availability of the medical doctors the women had the following suggestions: presence of medical doctors on 24×7 in the primary health centres/CHCs from 6 pm to 8 pm and nurses to stay in the same place during specified working hours, availability of free basic medicines for various ailments all the time. A few women from Karnataka felt that organizations like Lions Club and Rotary Club to conduct health check-up camps for one month annually for all members with different types of ailments. The Institute of Social Sciences can also organize health awareness programmes for one entire month once a year on a regular basis with proper follow-up. Representatives specifically mentioned the extension of the medical insurance scheme for all women irrespective of the age-group. In addition, women are willing to contribute ₹100 annually as part of health insurance from the community side provided they don't have to pay from their own reserves during an illness. Further they also felt that the public hospital should be as competent as the private hospitals, so that poor women do not end up being enticed by the private hospitals.

Thus, panchayat women can play a more active role in many new initiatives to be taken and to participate in the decision-making mechanism and to address the challenges of health finances and health resource policies. Therefore, better delivery of health services is available not only for girls but also for all women living in rural areas.

On 26th April the EWRs from the study areas of UN Women such as Odisha, Andhra Pradesh, Karnataka, Rajasthan and Madhya Pradesh met to further deliberate on the challenges facing them while working in the panchayats and what can be done to override those. Unfortunately, women from Andhra Pradesh were only motivators and not elected members since the panchayat election is still to take place. However, whenever they intervened, they seemed to be aware of the provisions of NRHM.

It was interesting to note that almost all the EWRs knew about the activities of ASHA in great detail. Even the newly elected EWRs from Odisha knew about the state variation of NRHM which is known as MAMTA. They talked about the Janani Express which is supposed to take the pregnant woman to the nearest hospital. But most of the time it is not available. One of them said that one pregnant woman gets ₹ 5,000 if she delivers her baby in the hospital. But her Bihari friend confided that her pregnant sister gets only ₹ 1,500. But the EWRs from both states agreed that most of the money is siphoned away by the doctors, nurses, and taxi drivers.

The EWRs from Karnataka as well as the motivators from Andhra Pradesh observed that ASHA not only helps pregnant women but also distributes sanitary napkins among the young women and spreads positive messages about HIV and AIDS.

Another interesting point that emerged from the meeting was that while the villagers from Jhabua district, MP did not accept the building of the toilets, the Sehore villagers went whole hog to adhere to clean sanitary practices; the reason being availability of water in both the districts.

EWRs from Rajasthan discussed the status of the standing committee. Some of them pointed out that the committee never meets. They also admitted that both Sahoyogini, the counterpart of ASHA and Anganwadi workers work together to meet the needs of the women and children. Finally each one of them showed concern that they were not aware of the amount of grants coming to each panchayat under the health scheme.

16

Gandhiji showed the Way*

Varsha Das

"I am sure you have heard a lot since morning about how to stay healthy and help others also to stay fit. You must have discussed the cleanliness of our body, our home, streets and the village." Varsha Das observed. Awareness of health includes hygiene, latrines, safe drinking water and safe refuse disposal. Women carry multiple burdens on their shoulders, literally as well as figuratively. To be able to give their best in all the areas of responsibility you must agree that they need to have a balanced and nutritious diet. However, we do know that there are so many of our brothers and sisters, children and aged who do not get even one square meal. Food, shelter and clothing are our basic needs, but even those are not available to everyone. We want health for all even in the midst of so much deprivation. This cannot be fulfilled by mere wishful thinking.

Mahatma Gandhi has mentioned in his book *The Health Guide*[1], "Only that man can be said to be really healthy who has a sound mind in a sound body. The relation between the body and the mind is so intimate that if either of them goes out of order the whole system would suffer". By man he meant humankind. Women are included. He adds, "We have to acquire the faculty of keeping well under all weathers—a difficult task. I know. But it is not beyond human reach. The mind plays a great part in it".

---

* Valedictory Address.

Gandhiji's words are absolutely true. I would like to share with you my own experience. My parents had lived a very happy married life for nearly fifty years. My father died after a brief illness. This created a sudden vacuum in my mother's life. On account of this unbearable pain in her life she suffered cerebral thrombosis. The left side of her body got paralyzed. My mother was a writer and a social worker. For an active person like her this paralysis was worse than death. She felt extremely helpless and defeated. Her mind was so depressed that she stopped using even the right side of the body, which was absolutely fine! All day and night she just wept.

At that point I brought her to Delhi to live with me. I started two fold treatment for her. According to the doctor's advice she began to take physiotherapy. Someone used to come home to give her regular exercises. And to bring joy back into her life, to turn her mind from negative to positive, I introduced her to a spiritual path that I have followed for many years. Gradually her mind changed from helplessness to hopefulness. I kept telling her that she should not feel sorry for herself, that she was already empowered to become healthy. She must keep telling herself that she would definitely regain her health. This worked. She gradually became a cheerful person. Her tears disappeared and her self-confidence returned. She began to use her right limbs. Now was the time to push her left limbs with the power of her mind. She did that and succeeded. Her paralysis did not disappear completely but she dragged her left foot and was able to walk with the help of a stick.

Our body has the power to heal, to fight the disease. It is said by a Japanese thinker Mr. Toda that our body is like a pharmaceutical factory. If we keep our mind strong and positive our body can produce the right kind of chemicals! We should certainly consult a doctor, but should also have a healthy mind.

The government provides many facilities and funds for various health programmes. We should be aware of them, and should use them for all those who need them. We also have to muster courage to expose and oppose any irregularity we notice in disbursing the funds and medical facilities. It has been noticed in some states that 80 per cent of medical facilities are availed of by only 20 per cent of the population! We do not benefit by mere announcements of schemes. We have to make them accessible to each person in the panchayat zone. This is our duty, and also a right. Let us challenge and overcome the obstacles, defeat the plans of avaricious middlemen by employing non-violent and courageous methods.

Gandhiji had mentioned in his journal *Harijan*, dated June 29, 1935, "It is health which is real wealth, not pieces of silver and gold". But what do we see around us? People ruin their health to collect more and more pieces of that glittering metal!

Before I conclude, I would like to draw your attention to an important aspect of development. Are we increasing unemployment in the name of development? Are we uprooting ourselves from the mother earth, i.e., from the eternal values of life? Have we become so self-centred and thick skinned that we are not even able to feel the pain of others? Are we destroying nature in the name of development? How can we remain healthy if we keep exploiting the earth, water, forest, air, etc., if we continue to pollute them? Our relationship with nature is an eternal continuum. Our lives are harmed if nature is harmed. We will be destroyed if nature is destroyed. Material gains have become more important than life itself. In the midst of all this we can and should create a healthy body, a healthy mind and a healthy society.

My mentor, Dr. Ikeda says, "Instead of one person taking 100 steps, let 100 people take one step together". He is talking about an inclusive approach which will create a healthy co-existence. Let us do our best to make it a success.

NOTES

1. M. K. Gandhi, (1942-44) *Key to Health.* Translated by Sushila Nair from Gujarati published by Navajivan Publishing House, Ahmedabad.

REFERENCES

Again it was compiled by Anand Hingorani, 1965.

About the Book: This small booklet is a manual or guide to health, is to be recommended for both, the choice of topic and its lucid presentation. This book is welcomed by common medicine enthusiasts, and students, alike. Gandhi wrote these chapters while he was confined in the Agakhan Palace at Poona during 1942-44. By writing this book, Gandhiji wanted to convey to his people and to the world the vital question of health. To him, a study of this question was part of the service of God and his creation, which was his mission.

This book was translated into many Indian and European languages. Gandhi wrote a few articles under the heading "Guide to Health" in 1906 in *Indian Opinion*, a weekly started by him, and later were published in a book form. He wrote this book as he had looked upon the problem of health from a novel point of view, somewhat different from the orthodox methods adopted by doctors and *vaidyas*.

The book also covers various aspects of health including the human body, air, water, food, *brahmacharya,* condiments, tea, coffee, cocoa, intoxicants, opium, and tobacco. The articles, though brief, are rich in content, and enable the reader to have a basic idea of health. Gandhi gave the name "Key to Health" and said anyone who observes the rules of health mentioned in the book will find that he would have the real key to unlock the gates, leading him (her) to good health. He (she) will not need to knock on doctors' or *vaidyas*' doors from day to day. (Editor).

17

Panchayats, Women and Health for All*

Almas Ali and *Bidyut Mohanty*

"I shall give you a talisman. When faced with the dilemma as to what your next step should be, remember the most wretched and vulnerable human beings you ever saw. The step you contemplate should help him" (her).

—Mahatma Gandhi

"The best form of providing health protection would be to change the economic system which produces ill health, and to liquidate ignorance, poverty and unemployment. The practice of each individual purchasing his (her) own medical care does not work. It is unjust, inefficient, wasteful and completely outmoded. In our highly geared, modern industrial society, there is no such thing as private health—all health is public. The illness and maladjustments of one unit of the mass affects all other members. The protection of people's health should be recognized by the government as its primary obligation and duty to its citizens."

Norman Bethune, 1936
cited in Reddy and Shiva Kumar, (2012)

---

* This was circulated as the Background Paper.

Introduction

After a gap of over forty years, between 1950 and 1992, it was realized by the policy makers of India that policies made in Delhi would not address the welfare of the people at the village level. The policies should be made in the villages which would reflect the needs of the local people. Hence, the reinvention of local government systems or panchayats with new roles by legislating a law in 1993 through amending the Constitution with a vision of bringing the clean and responsive administration to people's doorsteps. That decision led the villagers to elect at least three million grassroots leaders in each term of five years, of which one million are women. The 73rd Amendment to the Constitution formalized Panchayati Raj Institutions (PRIs) in the village, at the intermediate and district level. The goal was to strengthen local level institutions to provide for representations of women, of weaker sections and enhance the effectiveness of developmental schemes. Panchayats are supposed to implement and monitor 29 subjects as per the Eleventh Schedule which include developmental issues such as sanitation, health including maternal health, shelter and food security.

The seminal ICSSR/ICMR report of 1981 categorically states the overall improvement in health conditions is only possible under the PRIs. This would rightly entrust the health and illness care to the people who understand the needs of their communities much better than anybody else. Unfortunately, the central role of panchayats that is to plan and execute the developmental agenda has not yet materialized.

In this chapter an effort will be made to show the status of women's health, health policy of India and role of panchayats in the area of health governance. In particular, we will discuss the bottlenecks which will be encountered to achieve health for all coverage that has been declared very early[1] and the government has announced to achieve universal health by 2020. The role of panchayats and elected women leaders in achieving universal health and problems thereby will also be taken up. It is important to discuss these issues now because at present there are 2.7 lakh PRIs with at least three million elected representatives of which one million elected women leaders who are in charge of looking after the welfare of the families as well as that of the villagers. Further it is important to discuss the synergy between two sets of institutions because the National Rural Health Mission is entering the second phase and also the government is trying to achieve the Millennium Development Goals by 2015. Finally, some recommendations to rectify bottlenecks will also be suggested.

Health Scenario and Equity Concerns in Health in India

India trails in health outcomes behind its South Asian neighbours such as Sri Lanka and Bangladesh, which have a comparable per capita income, though India has made considerable progress with respect to improving the health of the people over the last forty years (from 1971 to 2010), which is reflected in the improvements in some of the health and demographic indicators presented below:

Fertility and Mortality Indicators: India (1971-2010)

Parameters	*1971*	*1981*	*1991*	*2001*	*Current (2010) (published in March 2012) Latest*
Crude Birth Rate (CBR)	36.9	38.0	35.0	28.2	22.1
Total Fertility Rate (TFR)	6.5	5.4	4.6	3.5	2.5
Crude Death Rate (CDR)	21.3	16.0	13.6	9.3	7.2
Infant Mortality Rate (IMR)	129	110	73	66	47

In India the need for a dependable demographic data was felt soon after independence. The Registration of Births and Deaths started on a voluntary basis and there was no uniformity in statistical returns resulting in both under-registration and incomplete coverage. In order to unify these civil registration activities, the Registration of Births and Deaths Act 1969 was enacted. Despite making the registration of births and deaths compulsory, the level of registration of births and deaths under the Act continued to be far from satisfactory in most of the states. With a view to generate reliable and continuous data on mortality and fertility indicators, the office of the RGI initiated the scheme of Sample Registration of Births and Deaths in India, popularly known as the Sample Registration System (SRS) in 1964-65 on a pilot basis and on full scale from 1969-70. Based on the dual record system, the SRS has been providing reliable estimates of mortality and fertility on a regular basis from 1971 onwards. The SRS data is considered to be the most reliable at the national level to be compared among the states at different points of time.

The Crude Birth Rate (CBR) has declined from 36.9 in 1971 to 22.1 in 2010 according to the latest SRS statistical report published in March 2012. The Total Fertility Rate (TFR) has declined from 6.5 in 1971 to 2.5 during the same period. The Crude Death Rate (CDR) has also fallen from 21.3 in 1971 to 7.2 in 2010. The Infant Mortality Rate (IMR), which was 129, has declined to 47 during the same period. Despite this overall improvement in health status, inequity in health exists and persists. It is well known that, poverty, gender, caste, tribe, geographical location and other social factors clearly affect the health status. Hence one notices the regional variations even though the overall picture has improved. As discussed below for minds prone to generalizations, India can prove to be a notorious quicksand and national averages can be quite misleading, because broad aggregates conceal the large disparities and wide variations, which exist between geographical regions, among states, within states, among districts, within districts, among Community Development (CD) Blocks, within Blocks, and particularly among social groups like Scheduled Tribes (STs), Scheduled Castes (SCs), Minorities, etc.

On top of it, low public spending on health (1% of GDP), high out-of-pocket payments (71%) leading to impoverishment, high levels of anaemia (56% among ever-married women aged 15-45 years) reflect in high levels of malnutrition among children (wasting 22.9%, stunting 44.9%), high infant mortality (47/1000 live births) and maternal mortality (212 per 1 lakh live births). Even though maternal mortality rate has declined on an average from 254 in 2004-2005 to 212 in 2007-09 India is still to reach the goal of Millennium Development Goal namely, 109 which is to be achieved in 2015[2]. Similarly, the infant mortality rate is about 47 per thousand births in 2010 at the all India level but the regional level variations would be too wide[3]. One-third of the world's malnourished children are in India according to the UN Report[4]. Along with the traditional diseases, new diseases place an undue burden on the poor and marginalized people of rural India. Equally worrying is the growing reliance on private providers, which currently service 78 per cent of out-patients and 60 per cent of in-patients. For those who cannot afford private services, illness translates into high out-of-pocket expenditure as a proportion of total household expenditure, reaching catastrophic proportions at times (i.e., equal to or greater than 40 per cent of a household's non-subsistence income).

Women's Health in India

The most glaring form of gender discriminations is in the health sector, where it is visibly manifested in the high level of sex differentials of high mortality and morbidity, low female to male ratio as well as differential access to treatment and care. However, conceptually a lot of ground has been gained with the positioning of women's health beyond the maternal roles and procreation. It has been unwaveringly stated that improvements in the access and availability of healthcare services are a necessary but not a sufficient condition to improve women's health. It is being increasingly recognized that women's health issues go much beyond maternal morbidity and mortality to include nutrition, child-bearing, abortion, reproductive health, Reproductive Tract Infections (RTIs), Sexually Transmitted Diseases (STDs) including HIV/AIDS, communicable diseases, violence against women, etc. Women face many health problems which are not linked to pregnancy. The leading causes of morbidity in women in rural India are non-specific fever, acidity, serious communicable diseases such as TB, malaria, weakness, dizziness, breathing problems and anaemia. In the present context, women live longer than men. But diseases of old age are never looked after by the policy makers.

Indian women often tolerate ill health without complaint. A number of community-based studies have brought to light that a considerable proportion of women suffer silently from a range of gynaecological problems. Women in India are affected by many of the same health conditions as men, but women experience them differently. The prevalence of poverty and economic dependence among women, their experience of violence, negative attitude of our society towards women and girls, limited power many women have over their sexual and reproductive lives and lack of influence in decision-making are some of the social realities which have an adverse impact on their health. Shortage of food and inequitable distribution of food for girls and women in the household, inadequate access to safe water, deficient housing conditions all overburden women and their families and have a negative impact/effect on their health.

As mentioned above the latest estimates of the maternal mortality ratio by the Registrar General of India, 2007-09, MMR for India stands at 212 per 1,00,000 live births. It constitutes 20 per cent of the total maternal mortality at the world level. At one end of the spectrum are states like Assam (390) followed by Uttar Pradesh (359), Rajasthan (318), MP (269), Bihar (261) and Odisha (258), which have high MMR, while at the other end of the spectrum are states like Kerala (81), Tamil Nadu (97), Maharashtra (104) and Gujarat (148), which have comparatively low MMR. It is estimated that for each woman who dies as many as 30 other women develop chronic and debilitating conditions, which seriously affect the quality of life. Nearly seven million induced abortions take place annually in India. For each legal abortion, it is estimated that another 10 illegal abortions take place, but go unrecorded. Nearly 12 per cent of all maternal deaths are attributable to abortion-related complications. Anaemia is the underlying cause for 20 per cent, toxemia for 13 per cent, puerperal sepsis for 13 per cent and bleeding during pregnancy for 23 per cent of maternal deaths. Maternal mortality is usually high in those states, where fertility is high, because there women have frequent pregnancies. Maternal mortality is also high in those states, where children are born to very young women and to women who have multiple and closely spaced pregnancies.

Structural Problems

Apart from inadequate funding, there are several other structural problems too, like, the lack of integration between disease control and other programmes in the social sector, sub-optimal use of traditional systems of medicines, weak regulatory systems for drugs as well as for medical practice, and poor capacity in public health management. A sound health system also requires the active participation of communities in preventive and promotive healthcare, on which the progress has been uneven. There is a strong mismatch between the declared objective of the universal healthcare through the public health system and public health expenditure in India. The mismatch between the objective and the resources is at the heart of the inadequacy and inequity of the Indian health system. (Kurian, 2011).[5] As mentioned earlier, the public expenditure on the health system hovers round just one per cent of the total GDP.

On Independence Day of 2011, the Prime Minister Mr. Manmohan Singh announced the significance of the health sector and declared that the Twelfth Five Year Plan would be the plan meant for health. The government wanted to increase the percentage share of the health sector from the previous level. According to the expert committee, the increase will be to the tune of 2.5 percentage of the total GDP from that of 1.3[6]. The expert committee also pointed out that per capita government spending on health shows a disturbing trend. Outpatient treatment accounted for 74 per cent of the private out-of-pocket expenditures. Medicines claim 72 per cent of the total private spending. (*ibid*).

Thus one sees that there are multi-fold problems facing the nation in terms of the health scenario. Now let us examine in what ways the panchayats are involved in providing healthcare services.

Panchayats as the Providers of Healthcare

According to the National Population Policy 2000 and National Health Policy 2002, the panchayats have an important role to implement the public health policies. The panchayats are supposed to be the decentralized centre of convergence of service delivery at the village level. The Planning Commission set up a Task Force in 2001 to go through the various involvements of the panchayats in relation to health. The Task Force noticed that the PRIs were not equipped to take on the monitoring and implementing of health related services nor was there any cognizance of such a role. The Task Force recommended five major programmes in which the three tiers of panchayats could implement. Those are Reproductive and Child Health (RCH), programme for vector-borne diseases, blindness, TB Control Programme, and ST/AIDS. Activities include identification of the people in need of services, monitoring the village level health workers, and Primary and Secondary healthcare facilities. (Bheenaveni Ramaaiah, 2012).[7] In 2001 the Central Council of Ministers of Health and Family Welfare resolved that the state governments should involve the PRIs in implementation of the health and family welfare programmes by progressive transfer of funds, functionaries and functions and by equipping them with capacity building measures. As a result, they could manage and supervise the activities of the healthcare and family welfare-related infrastructures suitably. These institutions should also coordinate the activities of the health-related block and village level functionaries[8].

In 2005, the overall objectives of the NRHM (which will be discussed a little below) included the pivotal role of panchayats along with health and the determinants of health for which inter-sectoral convergence of various departments such as PRIs, Women and Child Development (WCD), Rural Water Supply and Sanitation (RWSS) and that of education, is essential[9]. In this Mission also panchayats are supposed to play a significant role in planning, implementing and monitoring the interventions included in the NRHM. The government wanted to fulfil the MDGs by 2015 by introducing the NRHM[10].

As of today, NRHM envisages the following roles for PRIs:

- Commitments for development for devolution of funds, functionaries and programmes.
- District Health Mission (DHM) to be led by the Zilla Parishad. The DHM will control, guide and manage all Public Health institutions in the district, CHC (Community Health Centres), PHCs and sub-centres.
- ASHA would be selected by and be accountable to the village panchayat.

- VHSC (GKS) would prepare the village health plan/GP health plan, promote inter-sectoral convergence.
- Each sub-centre will have an untied fund for local action @ ₹ 10,000 per annum. This fund will be deposited in a joint bank account of ANM and sarpanch and operated by ANM with consultation with VHSC/GKS.
- PRI involvement in Rogi Kalyan Samiti (RKS) for good hospital management.
- Making available health-related databases to all stakeholders, including panchayats at all levels.

Again according to the vision document of the 11th Five Year Plan, 2007-2012, it is envisaged that health issues can be taken up more effectively by involving Panchayati Raj Institutions (PRIs) and civil society organizations. Both these would work to implement the schemes keeping the transparency accountability in mind. It would be easy to get feedback from the community regarding the efficacy of the scheme. It was also envisaged that irregularities could be checked by using the Right to Information which was introduced in 2005[11]. According to 11th Schedule, panchayats are supposed to be in charge of implementing and monitoring health issues. Since the reservation at the panchayat level has thrown up a large number of women representatives, and women are in charge of health of the family as well as that of villagers, one would have noticed the women as the active health workers as well. But as we will see later, how panchayats have been sidelined.

The Twelfth Plan Steering Committee Report rightly recognizes the important and pivotal role that local self-government bodies can play in improving health. According to the report: Local self-government bodies which have a constitutional mandate and are accountable to the people are the *natural forums* for achieving convergence in health. Such convergence should translate into a quicker and more holistic approach for line item subjects falling across different departments. An illustrative list of line ministries and corresponding PRI functions Impacting Health has been mapped in the form of an exhaustive table highlighting the role of PRIs as natural forums for convergence in the field. The mandate of Village Health and Sanitation Committee—VHSC (called Gaon Kalyan Samiti—GKS in Odisha) has been recently promoted to include Nutrition (VHSNC) and recognized as a sub-committee of the panchayat. Public health needs many actions from individuals, family and community for their own well-being and the well-being of others in the community. This fact needs to be emphasized so that municipal bodies and panchayats take the responsibility in their local areas as mandated in the 73rd and 74th constitutional amendments. In fact, the Bajaj Committee (1996) had recommended the health services at CHC/PHC/sub-centre would be interested to serve the PRIs, while the midterm review of the Eleventh Plan had suggested empowerment of PRIs to perform the functions entrusted to them. Whatever be the new form the public health management by PRI takes, they would have to be empowered with administrative and financial power and human and financial resources. The PRI's capacity to play a meaningful role in planning and execution of Public Health functions need to be carefully supported.

In practice, even though health is one of the subjects divested to the panchayats, the panchayats are excluded completely. In the guidelines of NRHM, it is clearly stated that each panchayat should chalk out the health plan. It is also stated that ASHA should be responsible to the chiefs of the panchayats. But in practice she is paid from the block level health functionaries and hence she is responsible to them. Further under the civic functions, panchayats are supposed to take up the sanitation, drinking water issues, reporting of the breakout of epidemics, etc. All these aspects are also health-related. NRHM has tried to rectify the weakness by making a provision to constitute the village health, sanitation and nutrition committee. The chief of the panchayat is also a member of the committee. But the committee is not answerable to the panchayats. Similarly, at the district level the District Health Mission will coordinate the NRHM functions. In practice, however, the district level medical officer is in charge of the health related functions. The role of implementing and monitoring the health related problems become futile if the funding is not routed through these institutions. The suggestions of the Steering Committee which are going to be implemented to strengthen the outcomes of the health policies, has highlighted the role of 'participatory governance'. Even here, the explicit role of PRIs are not mentioned though the role of the gram sabha in the form of community participation is highlighted (Annexure IV and V).

There are many field studies conducted to show that panchayats play a minor role in implementing the flagship programme like NRHM because of paucity of funds, functionaries and power. As for example, Vyusulu Poornima and Vijayalaksmi[12] have taken up surveys in two districts of Karnataka and have shown that there is hardly any linkage between the panchayats and health department. The authors have taken up two districts and have interviewed women in panchayats, pregnant women and common women to get their results. The women in panchayats do not get any information regarding health facilities. The authors point out that even though the women wish to have the delivery in the hospital facilities are not available and they are compelled to go to private clinics.

Sometimes it is alleged that panchayat representatives are not aware of the health issues and do not take any interest in attending to the health problems of the village. But it is noticed that after getting exposure from the civil society the elected women representatives take up implementing the Janani Surakshya Yojana and encourage the pregnant women to visit the primary health centre. This was the finding of the Institute of Social Sciences, New Delhi which had taken up an evaluation task of the five states where the UNDP had supported the programme of Capacity Building of EWRs from reservation to representation. The states covered were UP, Chhattisgarh, MP, Bihar and Rajasthan. It is also encouraging to note that some of the potential women candidates contesting for panchayat election in Odisha are from the background of having work experience in the anganwadi centre. It is hoped that these women will show more interest in health issues of the local areas[13].

Still newly elected members of PRIs, especially women members, having no experience in public affairs need support as they enter into their new roles. There is a need to draw an integrated curriculum addressing comprehensive health and health determinants of non-health sectors and design training courses for local self-government body functionaries (PRIs and ULBs), especially women across the country.

The Health Policy of India

The Directive Principles of the State Policy in the Constitution of India mandate improvement of public health as one of the primary duties of the state. Health for all means that health is to be brought within reach of everyone including the poorest members of the society in the remotest areas. And by "health is meant not just the availability of health services but a personal well-being and a state of health that enables a person to lead a socially and economically productive life. "Health for all" implies the removal of the obstacles to health—that is to say, the elimination of malnutrition, ignorance, contaminated drinking water, and unhygienic housing—quite as much as it means the solution of problems such as a lack of doctors, hospital beds, drugs and vaccines. The main strategies for achieving health for all are: raising sufficient financial resources for the health of the country as a whole, reducing the financial risks and barriers to decrease the share of out-of-pocket expenses to the healthcare of the private households[14].

From time to time, the health policy of India has also been declared as the right of every human being. The notion of right started as early as 1946 with the Bhore Committee and even now the recommendations of the High Level Expert Groups which presented its recommendations on Access to Universal Healthcare in 2010, has echoed the same concern. (Rao, 2011)[15]

The Eleventh Five Year Plan Document 2008, acknowledged certain achievements such as India has achieved many successes namely, eradication of smallpox, leprosy, polio, and TB. There is a steady increase of life expectancy at birth. But there are several other problems haunting the nation such as widespread malnutrition among the children, high maternal mortality, and high infant mortality as we have discussed earlier. A very high proportion of population in the rural areas lack access to affordable healthcare[16]. These problems need to be addressed by multiple interventions most of which go beyond the curative healthcare facilities. Those factors are dietary improvement, nutrition supplements for children, better child care practices, access to safe drinking water, improved sanitation, and immunization, etc., the Plan document indicated. At the same time, it is also noticed that the out-of-pocket expenditure is also increasing. So keeping these considerations in mind, the government introduced the National Rural Health Mission (NRHM) in 2005. Secondly, the Planning Commission set up a High Level Expert Committee in 2010, with a mandate of developing a framework providing an easily accessible and affordable healthcare to all Indians. The high level expert committee was set up in 2010 and has submitted the findings in 2011. In the next section, the components of different health schemes will be discussed.

First we will take up the NRHM. In all related health policies a holistic approach towards health has been adopted to improve the health conditions of the millions of people who are still in the margin.

National Rural Health Mission (NRHM)

The National Rural Health Mission (NRHM) was introduced in 2005. The main objective of the NRHM is to provide accessible, affordable, and accountable quality health services, even to the poorest households in the remotest areas. The thrust of the Mission was to establish a fully functional community-owned decentralized health delivery system. Another aspect of the Mission is to have the inter-sectoral convergence at all levels, to ensure simultaneous action on a wide range of determinants of health such as, sanitation, education, nutrition, social and gender equality. It was also envisaged that it would have institutional integration with the fragmented health sector to provide a focus on outcomes, measured against Indian public health standards for all health facilities. The NRHM has shifted its focus from being a scheme to a functional health system at all levels from village to the district involving community and health functionaries at each level. As mentioned above, various institutional platforms of Village Health and Sanitation Committee, the Rogi Kalyan Samities, and PRIs have been envisaged to provide opportunities for convergent action on all determinants of health.

According to the objectives of the health scheme, NRHM promises to provide universal access to equitable, affordable and quality healthcare which is accountable and at the same time responsive to the needs of the people, especially those who are marginalized and live in rural areas. It also aims to make necessary architectural corrections to basic healthcare systems, reduce regional imbalances, pool resources, integrate organizational structures, optimize human resources, decentralize management of district health programmes and integrate many vertical health programmes. It aimed to facilitate community participation, partnership and ownership of health and healthcare delivery. Keeping that in mind, the following infrastructures have been created.

Sl. No.	*Infrastructure/Human Resource*	*Year 2005*	*Year 2010*
1.	No. of sub-centres	1,46,026	1,47,069
2.	No. of sub-centres in government buildings	63901	84957
3.	No. of PHCs	23236	23673
4.	PHCs in government buildings	16023	20236
5.	Doctors at PHC	20308	24085
6.	No. of CHCs	3346	4535
7.	Specialist in CHCs	3550	6781
8.	No. of nurses in PHCs and CHCs	28730	58450
9.	No. of pharmacists at PHCs and CHCs	17708	21688
10.	No. of laboratory technicians at PHCs and CHCs	12284	15094
11.	No. of radiographers at CHCs	1337	1817

1.	Rogi Kalyan Samitis	570 DHs, 4210 CHCs 1125 other than CHC hospitals above CHC level but below DH level, 16920 PHCs, 6795 other health facilities above SC but below block level have their own Rogi Kalyan Samitis with untied funds for improving quality of health services.
2.	ASHAs	8.61 lakh ASHAs selected, 2.55 lakhs trained upto the 5th module and 5.53 lakhs with drug kits in their respective villages.
3.	Village Health and Sanitation Committees	4.95 lakh (nearly 77%) have their own Village Health and Sanitation Committees. All of them have received the ₹ 10,000 untied grant for local action.
4.	Village Health and Nutrition Days	35.06 lakhs in 2006-07, 49.62 lakhs in 2007-08, 58.19 lakhs in 2008-09, 56.20 lakhs in 2009-10 and 8.45 lakhs in 2010-11. Village Health and Nutrition Days organized at ICDS centre to reach basic health services.

Source: NRHM website.

The other components of NRHM are: Promotion of public and private partnerships for achieving the public health goals and mainstreaming AYUSH—revitalizing local health traditions. It is a flagship programme of the central government and this year the budget allocation has increased by 15 per cent of the previous year. The amount for the year 2011-12 has been increased from 15 crore rupees to 20 crore rupees[17].

Yet another component of the NRHM is the Janani Surakshya Yojana (JSY). It is a demand-driven intervention. ASHA is in charge of tracking down the pregnant women and to persuade them to go to the nearest hospital for early check-up and to deliver the babies. In many states the local programme on a similar line has achieved some success. The Twelfth Plan recommends that the existing institutional framework under NRHM may be followed and expanded into a National Health Mission for providing services in both urban and rural areas.

Patterns of Health Expenditures at the State Level Implications for Universal Health Coverage

Health expenditures as a percentage of total expenditure on the health sector by the government have shown a continuous declining trend. The high income states such as Maharashtra, Punjab, Haryana, and Gujarat have continuously shown a continuous decline in health expenditure. In contrast, the middle and low income states like Andhra Pradesh, Arunachal Pradesh, Assam, Bihar, Himachal Pradesh, Madhya Pradesh, Rajasthan, and West Bengal have shown a rise in health expenditure till 1998 and then a continuous decline. Some of the low income states like Kerala, Tamil Nadu, Odisha and UP have followed the pattern of high income states. Percentage-wise some of the rich states spend very little such as 2.59 percentage of the total expenditure in Haryana to 3.5 in Maharashtra. (Hansa Jain, 2010)[18]. In other words, at the onset of the reforms period, the share of public expenditure has been declining and that of private share has increased.

Percentage of State-wise Public Expenditure on Health—2005

Himachal Pradesh	37.8
Assam	30.9
Rajasthan	30.4
Karnataka	28.9
UP	7.5
Haryana	10.4
Bihar	11.8
Kerala	12.9

Source: GoI, 2005 National Health Accounts for India, 2001-02.

Total Per Capita Private Expenditure on Health

Kerala	₹ 1858
Haryana	₹ 1570
Punjab	₹ 1530
UP	₹ 1124
Andhra Pradesh	₹ 1039
Odisha	₹ 582
Rajasthan	₹ 597
Karnataka	₹ 712

Source: GoI, 2005 National Health Accounts for India, 2001-02.

Andhra Pradesh		Haryana		Karnataka		Kerala		Odisha		Punjab		Rajasthan		U P	
Pub	Pvt	Pub	Pvt	Pub	Pvt	Pub	Pvt	Pub	Pvt	Pub	Pvt	Pub	Pvt	Pub	Pvt
%	(₹)	%	(₹)	%	(₹)	%	(₹)	%	(₹)	%	(₹)	%	(₹)	%	(₹)
	1039	10.4	1570	28.9	712	12.9	1858		582		1530	30.4	597	7.5	1124

Source: GoI, 2005 National Health Accounts for India, 2001-02.

According to the National Sample Surveys (NSS) of 1986-87, 1995-96, and 2004 on morbidity and use of healthcare services, it is noticed that the percentages of non-treatment of various illness and discontinuation of treatment has increased considerably in the last two decades because of financial reasons. According to the NSS office, 2006 more than 40 per cent of the poor patients have to borrow money for the treatment and 35 per cent of them fall into the Below Poverty Line. (Sen, 2012) In addition, there are differences between rural and urban in terms of availability of health resources. As for example, 80 per cent of the doctors, 75 per cent of the dispensaries and 60 per cent of the hospitals are located in the urban areas. (*ibid.*)

Universal Health Coverage (UHC)

In the above section, it is noticed that the out-of-pocket-expenditure has increased by leaps and bounds. At the same time the government spending has declined. Bearing that in mind the Steering Committee[19] has recommended the affordable healthcare by ensuring cashless treatment to one and all. In the words of Reddy and Kumar (2012),[20] "It is time to recognize that everyone and not just the poor, need to be protected against rising health costs that can impoverish any family". Universal coverage will greatly reduce out-of-pocket expenditure and provide much needed relief to the people". Thus the guiding principles of the UHC are the following: Those principles are based on universality, equity, non-exclusion, non-discrimination, comprehensive care with good quality. In addition, it is also envisaged to protect the financial stability as well as the rights of the patients. Reddy *et al.* also suggested that essential medicines and diagnostic essentials should be provided free of cost. The experts of the High Level Group (HLEG) recommended creating a 'national interoperable Health Information Network' to improve the governance, accountability, portability, storage of health records and managements. Investments in the areas of sanitation, safe drinking water, nutrition and livelihood provisions should be stepped up. Steps are to be taken to consolidate the public health provisioning and community participation. Further, the cooperation of strengthened public services and private partnership was also thought of. The document reiterated the objectives of NRHM to focus on the preventive, promotive and curative aspects of health services. The other components of the UHC are the following. The financial burden should be borne by the government by raising the budgetary provision. Secondly, the healthcare delivery institutions should be strengthened and the quality of health personnel should be improved. The HELG discussed the limitations of the private sector being the provider of healthcare services because of asymmetry of knowledge on the part of the patient and secondly intra-family discriminations against women and children in accessing the healthcare services. However, the group suggested that the public sector should contract in the private sectors with a pre-determined package. (Reddy and Kumar, 2012).

But as it will be pointed out, in the next section, the universal health coverage policy may not work effectively because of some shortcomings.

Critiquing the Health Policy

The main problem of the health policy is that so little is being spent on the health sector even though the Twelfth Plan has been declared as the Plan for health. As the editorial of *The Hindu* (2012)[21] points out the global average of hospital beds to the population is 2.9 per thousand, but in India it is only 0.9. It is also suggested that if the objective is on the preventive side, then a lower ratio that is two per thousand will be adequate. But half the beds available in the public hospital are listed as non-functional. Further the universal health coverage may not work well since the private sector is not well regulated.

Coupled with that the success of the NRHM is hampered with other problems. As for example, the health systems in terms of medicine, doctors, etc., fail quite frequently in the rural areas. Further the transport system is also very poor and the bad roads add to complicate the matter further. Women are referred to from one hospital to another till they reach a far flung medical college hospital. By that time they would have spent a considerable amount of money and time to get some treatment[22]. An organization called Obstetric and Gynaecological Society of India (FOGSI) has done a review of maternal deaths, in different states in November 2010 to March 2012. They have noticed that 90 per cent of the deaths occurring during their visit to hospitals at the time of delivery takes place in the transit period between two hospitals or between hospital and home. The woman gets financial incentives if she delivers the baby in the hospital. But generally the hospitals are overloaded with patients and so the woman is sent back home as soon she delivers the baby. In the process the mother lacks the proper post-natal treatment (*The Hindu,* 2012). The entire emphasis of the NRHM is focused on the reduction of maternal mortality apart from the women of the other age cycle such as old and young. Further it was envisaged that ASHA would work as the agent of change but due to excessive emphasis on the curative healthcare she has been reduced to an extended arm of the health service system[23].Again the background of ASHA is considered to be service-minded and sometimes they are appointed to get some remuneration. The army of Accredited Social Health Activists (ASHA) with a strong referral link with the health system will put extreme pressure to deliver the health services.[24]

On the other hand, the remuneration of ASHA is very low and does not provide any stimulus to work with sincerity. Apart from the above weaknesses, the government's erroneous policies have contributed to the ill health of women to which we turn next.

State Population Policies and the Two Child Norm

Several state governments have already formulated their state-specific population policies. There is a distinct difference in tone and attitude between the NPP and some of the state population policies. Some of the state policies reflect the neo-Malthusian "population control" mindset viewing population growth as a human crisis and are more upfront in methods of achieving demographic goals through a series of incentives and disincentives, and short-cut vertical programmes and strategies.

There is enough data and documentation to establish that disincentives tend to be coercive. It has also been noticed that the disincentives always hit the poor and underprivileged, especially those who belong to scheduled castes and tribes and backward classes.

It has been pointed out repeatedly by research scholars that the two-child norm (introduced in some states of India) is *anti-women*, anti-adivasi, anti-Dalit, anti-child and anti-poor in general. This is profoundly violative of human and democratic rights.

The 73rd and 74th Constitutional Amendment sought to strengthen and expand the base for India's democratic governance by providing constitutional recognition to local self-governance bodies. The states' legislation on Panchayati Raj providing disqualification on the basis of the two-child norm, invariably cite the National Population policy as the rationale for such a restrictive and punitive measure for elected representatives of the panchayats, when the National Population Policy does not provide such a norm.

An exploratory study on 'Panchayati Raj and Two-Child Norm: Implications and Consequences' was taken up by the Mahila Chetna Manch in the states of Andhra Pradesh, Haryana, Madhya Pradesh, Orissa and Rajasthan. This study found that its implementation is discriminatory to women and disadvantaged sections of the society. The study also clearly revealed that the economically and socially vulnerable sections are most affected by this legislation which is often misused to settle political scores or prevent the under privileged from getting into positions of power.

In the states where these laws have been imposed scores of cases have been documented, where women have been deserted or forced to undergo sex-selective abortions. Children have also been abandoned or given up for adoption. In general, such a norm provides an impetus for an increase in sex-selective abortions worsening the already existing dismal child sex ratio in the country.

Conclusions

The whole aim of PRIs is to bring clean, responsive and accountable administration to the doorstep of the villagers. These institutions are supposed to have control over the 29 subjects among which health, sanitation, nutrition, etc., constitute major components. These institutions are supposed to plan and implement the provisions of healthcare services, in coordination with health personnel of the respective tiers of panchayats. But in practice the lines department functionaries do not pay any attention to the elected representatives at all. In the language of the Ministry of Health and Family Welfare:

"There are enough portents to suggest that PRI engagement in improving key health indicators will become a reality. However in order to expedite the process and to make it more effective, consideration of key issues related to empowerment of panchayats through funds, human resources and capacity are critical. PRI engagement is perhaps the only existing mechanism to achieve large-scale community participation and reach the marginalized and vulnerable, particularly women, children, and the poor. Locating NRHM functions within the gram panchayat and implementing it through a village health committee/gram sabha will facilitate the process and make health for all an achievable reality." *(op. cit.)*

Coupled with that even though the new health policies have the dimensions of the rights-based approach and that of equity as well, it is riddled with many problems.

Involvement of the elected representatives and that of panchayats in health governance can significantly increase the motivation, performance and accountability of community health workers. It can also contribute to the much-needed convergence of social services at the community level. For this to happen, local health functions and finances should be devolved to PRIs and local bodies with clear directives and guidelines. The participation of PRIs and other elected representatives in health governance and community oversight through the (village and block) Health and Sanitation Committees has been generally inadequate due to operational deficits including low capacities and role of ambiguity. These gaps should be addressed through better training, role definition, financial devolution, capacity strengthening and the establishment of mechanisms through Health Assemblies for greater community oversight. NGOs should additionally be engaged to train PRI representatives in health administration (Annexure V).

Recommendations

1. The centrality of the panchayats in relation to devolving power, funds and management of health issues should be done.
2. The experimental universal health coverage of giving access

to generic medicine for one district should be extended to all the districts keeping very high out-of-pocket expenditure on health.

3. The experiment of the Tamil Nadu health delivery system namely, procuring and distributing medicine in a cost-effective manner should be adopted as one of the models which can be emulated in other states.
4. The centre should show the political will to achieve the health for all by 2015 by raising the share of health from 0.1 per cent to 0.5 per cent of GDP on drug security.
5. The public investment has to be targeted and prioritized, in the areas of needs for both the patients and facilities particularly in the tribal areas in terms of access to basic healthcare facilities.
6. Instead of expanding the number of health centres by 1.75 lakh units to reduce the maternal mortality 20,000 to 30,000 health units should be set up with all the equipment. In other words, instead of thinly spreading the health units, the government should set up a few with all the facilities to tackle the maternal mortality.
7. In order to provide the best outcome out of the proposed scheme the first step is to undertake a mapping of the health facilities and develop different financing models to achieve those goals.
8. The complex tension between the vertical and horizontal approach to managing the important disease control programmes should be resolved.
9. Women in panchayats should be given the role of planning and implementing the health related schemes.
10. There is an urgent need to inform, sensitize and motivate the members of panchayats on health issues. This calls for certain levels of specific expertise and skills.

REFERENCES

1. In 1946 the Bhore Committee Report had declared that to get health

treatment is a fundamental right for every individual. *Rao, Sujatha (2012)* "Long on Aspiration, Short on Detail: Report on Universal Health Coverage", *Economic and Political Weekly*. Vol. xlvii, No. 6.

2. http://www.censusindia.gov.in/vital_statistics/SRS_Bulletins/Final-MMR%20Bulletin-2007-09_070711.pdf
3. www.google.co.in/public .data
4. The Hindu, http://www.hindu.com,2006
5. Kurian , N. J. (2012) 'Issues in Health and Equity in India'in Mohanty, Manoranjan (ed) *India Social Development Report* (2010), New Delhi. Oxford University Press.
6. *The Times of India* November, 19, 2011 Delhi edition.
7. Bheenaveny, Ramaiah, (2012) 'Enhancing Services of Panchayat Raj in Public Health' http://www.scipolicy.net/enhancing-services-ofpanchayat -raj-in public -health/
8. http://mohfw.nic.in/NRHM/Exe_sum_PRI_health_min.htm
9. http://203.193.146.66/hfw/NRHM.asp?GL=7
10. http://mohfw.nic.in/NRHM/Documents/5_Years_NRHM_Final.pdf
11. Government of India, Eleventh Five Year Plan-2007-2012, Vol. 1 Inclusive Growth (Planning Commission, 2008).
12. Vyusulu, P. and Vijayalakshmi, 'Reproductive Health Services, and Role of Panchayats in Karnataka'http://www. isec.ac.in/ Karnataka_Poornima_Vijayalakshmi_aligned.pdf
13. I personally visited some of the panchayats in the Koojang block in Jagatsinghpur District during the time of the recent panchayat election and talked to some of the women candidates who were contesting the election.
14. Mahal, Ajay and Victoria Fan (2011), "Achieving Universal Coverage in India : An Assessment of the Policy Challenge" (Occasional paper, Draft) http://www.ncaer.org/popuppages/EventDetails/IPF_2011/ Ajay_Mahal&Victoria_Fan.pdf
15. Rao, Sujatha, (2012), 'Long on Aspirations , Short on Detail: Report on Universal Health Coverage.' *Economic and Political Weekly*, Vol. XLVII, No.6, p. 12.
16. *Ibid*.
17. http://zeenews.india.com/news/health/exclusive/better-health-services-for-poor-envisaged_16075.html
18. Jain Hansa (2010) 'Health Sector Reforms and Health Poverty' *Social Change*, Vol. 40, Number 1, March.
19. The Steering Committee was set up during the finalization of theTwelfth Five Year Plan to provide affordable healthcare to all by strengthening the NRHM.

20. Reddy, Srinath K. Shiva Kumar (2012), 'The Road to Universal Healthcare', *The Hindu*, April 14, 2012 (Delhi edition).
21. *The Hindu*, March 21, 2012 (Delhi edition) editorial page.
22. Human Rights Watch.
23. Joshi, Sujay and Mathew George (2012), 'Healthcare through Community Participation: Role of ASHA', *Economic and Political Weekly*, Vol. XLV11, No. 10.
24. Government of India (2005), *National Rural Health Mission: Meeting People's Health Needs in Rural Areas*. Ministry of Health and Family Welfare, New Delhi.

Annexure - I

Millennium Development Goals: India

- Goal 1. Eradicate extreme poverty and hunger
  - Target 1. Halve, between 1990 and 2015, the proportion of people whose income is less than one dollar a day
    - Poorest quintile's share in national income or consumption, per cent (WB).
    - Population below $1 (PPP) per day consumption, percentage.
    - Population below national poverty line, rural, percentage.
    - Population below national poverty line, total, percentage.
    - Population below national poverty line, urban, percentage.
    - Poverty gap ratio.
    - Purchasing power parities (PPP) conversion factor, local currency unit to international dollar.
  - Target 2. Halve, between 1990 and 2015, the proportion of people who suffer from hunger
    - Children under 5 moderately or severely underweight, percentage.
    - Children under 5 severely underweight, percentage.
    - Population undernourished, number of people.
    - Population undernourished, percentage.
- Goal 2. Achieve universal primary education
  - Target 3. Ensure that, by 2015, children everywhere,

boys and girls alike, will be able to complete a full course of primary schooling

- Literacy rates of 15-24 years old, both sexes, percentage.
- Literacy rates of 15-24 years old, men, percentage.
- Literacy rates of 15-24 years old, women, percentage.
- Net enrolment ratio in primary education, both sexes.
- Net enrolment ratio in primary education, boys.
- Net enrolment ratio in primary education, girls.
- Percentage of pupils starting grade 1 reaching grade 5, both sexes.
- Percentage of pupils starting grade 1 reaching grade 5, boys.
- Percentage of pupils starting grade 1 reaching grade 5, girls.
- Primary completion rate, both sexes.
- Primary completion rate, boys.
- Primary completion rate, girls.

- Goal 3. Promote gender equality and empower women
  - Target 4. Eliminate gender disparity in primary and secondary education, preferably by 2005, and to all levels of education not later than 2015
    - Gender Parity Index in primary level enrolment.
    - Gender Parity Index in secondary level enrolment.
    - Gender Parity Index in tertiary level enrolment.
    - Seats held by men in national Parliament.
    - Seats held by women in national Parliament, percentage.
    - Share of women in wage employment in the non-agricultural sector.
    - Total number of seats in national Parliament.

  - Women to men parity index, as ratio of literacy rates, 15-24 years old.
- Goal 4. Reduce child mortality
  - ➢ Target 5. Reduce by two thirds, between 1990 and 2015, the under-five mortality rate
    - Children 1 year-old immunized against measles, percentage.
    - Children under five mortality rate per 1,000 live births.
    - Infant mortality rate (0-1 year) per 1,000 live births.
- Goal 5. Improve maternal health
  - ➢ Target 6. Reduce by three quarters, between 1990 and 2015, the maternal mortality ratio
    - Births attended by skilled health personnel, percentage.
    - Maternal mortality ratio per 100,000 live births.
- Goal 6. Combat HIV/AIDS, malaria and other diseases
  - ➢ Target 7. Have halted by 2015 and begun to reverse the spread of HIV/AIDS
    - Condom use at last high-risk sex, 15-24 years old, men, percentage.
    - Condom use at last high-risk sex, 15-24 years old, women, percentage.
    - Condom use to overall contraceptive use among currently married women 15-49 years old, percentage.
    - Contraceptive use among currently married women 15-49 years old, any method, percentage.
    - Contraceptive use among currently married women 15-49 years old, condom, percentage.
    - Contraceptive use among currently married women 15-49 years old, modern methods, percentage.

- Men 15-24 years old with comprehensive correct knowledge of HIV/AIDS, percentage.
- Men 15-24 years old, who know that a person can protect himself from HIV infection by consistent condom use, percentage.
- People living with HIV, 15-49 years old, percentage.
- Women 15-24 years old with comprehensive correct knowledge of HIV/AIDS, percentage.
- Women 15-24 years old, who know that a person can protect himself from HIV infection by consistent condom use, percentage.

➢ Target 8. Have halted by 2015 and begun to reverse the incidence of malaria and other major diseases

- Tuberculosis death rate per 100,000 population.
- Tuberculosis detection rate under DOTS, percentage.
- Tuberculosis prevalence rate per 100,000 population.
- Tuberculosis treatment success rate under DOTS, percentage.

- Goal 7. Ensure environmental sustainability

➢ Target 9. Integrate the principles of sustainable development into country policies and programmes and reverse the loss of environmental resources

- Carbon dioxide emissions (CO_2), metric tonnes of CO_2 per capita (CDIAC).
- Carbon dioxide emissions (CO_2), thousand metric tonnes of CO_2 (CDIAC).
- Consumption of all Ozone-Depleting Substances in ODP metric tonnes.
- Consumption of ozone-depleting CFCs in ODP metric tonnes.
- Energy use (Kg oil equivalent) per $1,000 (PPP) GDP.

  - Land area covered by forest, percentage.
  - Protected area to total surface area, percentage.
  - Protected areas, sq. km.
- ➢ Target 10. Halve by 2015 the proportion of people without sustainable access to safe drinking water
  - Proportion of the population using improved drinking water sources, rural.
  - Proportion of the population using improved drinking water sources, total.
  - Proportion of the population using improved drinking water sources, urban.
  - Proportion of the population using improved sanitation facilities, rural.
  - Proportion of the population using improved sanitation facilities, total.
  - Proportion of the population using improved sanitation facilities, urban.
- ➢ Target 11. By 2020 to have achieved a significant improvement in the lives of at least 100 million slum dwellers
  - Slum population as percentage of urban, percentage.
  - Slum population in urban areas

- Goal 8. Develop a global partnership for development in the long term
  - Debt service as percentage of exports of goods and services and net income from abroad.
- ➢ Target 16. In cooperation with developing countries, develop and implement strategies for decent and productive work for youth
- ➢ Target 18. In cooperation with the private sector, make available the benefits of new technologies, especially information and communications
  - Internet users.

- Internet users per 100 population.
- Personal computers.
- Personal computers per 100 population.
- Telephone lines and cellular subscribers.
- Telephone lines and cellular subscribers per 100 population.

Source: United Nations Statistics Division—Unless otherwise noted, information in this page is accurate as of February 15, 2007.

Annexure - II

Reviving Local Health Traditions

Darshan Shankar, Abdul Hafeel, Unnikrishnan Payyappapallimana and *Suma Tagadur, FRLHT, India*

The mission of FRLHT, the Foundation for the Revitalisation of Local Health Traditions, is to revitalise the local practices, beliefs and customs related to health in four states of Southern India. People in India have an outstanding knowledge of medicinal plants acquired over centuries, and in the majority of rural communities illness is treated with home remedies and by specialised folk healers.Yet, such knowledge and practices are eroding rapidly under the influence of modernisation. One of the main objectives of the FRLHT-Compas programme is to document and rapidly assess specific remedies. An innovative methodology was developed, in which local healers were supported, and selected local practices were compared with western bio-medicine as well as other codified medical systems, such as Ayurveda, Siddha and Unani.

Local health traditions are practices, beliefs and customs related to health, specific to each locality and passed on from generation to generation by word of mouth. They make use of a surprisingly wide array of locally available flora and fauna. Thousands of specialized folk healers are versed in methods such as pulse diagnosis, examination of urine, specific poison treatment, and *varma kalai*, diagnosis and treatment using 'vital points' in the body.

Codified Medical Systems in India

Local health traditions can be found throughout India parallel to codified or classical systems of medicine. These codified systems consist of medical knowledge, which includes sophisticated theoretical foundations expressed in thousands of manuscripts. Apart form western bio-medicine, examples in India are Ayurveda, Siddha, Unani and the Tibetan tradition. Siddha is one of the oldest systems of medicine in India, largely therapeutic in nature and specialised in pharmacology. Its principles and doctrines are similar to Ayurveda. The Unani system, with its origin in Greece, was introduced by the Arabs and Persians around the eleventh century. Unani interacts closely with Ayurveda and other local medical systems. Tibetan medicine in India is primarily a regional manifestation of Ayurveda. It is estimated that there are 600,000 licensed medical practitioners of these codified systems of medicine.

Local Health Traditions in India

Traditional healers.In addition to these codified systems, there are over a million community-based traditional health workers, including 60,000 village bone setters, 60,000 herbal medicine practitioners (excluding spiritual healers) specialising in jaundice, paralytic conditions, children's diseases, eye diseases, poison healing, dentistry, etc., and around 700,000 midwives in India [Shankar, 1992]. These are India's traditional barefoot doctors, or *Nattu Vaidyas*. They assist in around 80 per cent of all rural deliveries, treat over 40 per cent of broken bones and 50 per cent of snake, scorpion and dog bites. Sophisticated therapeutic techniques include *marmam* (treatment of vital points), *agni* and *kshara karma* (cauterization), *sodhanakarma* (purificatory techniques), *rasayana* (rejuvenative therapy), techniques used in the management of dislocated joints, as well as surgical management of a number of conditions. They also treat health problems in domestic animals.

Traditional healers do not undertake medical service as a full-time vocation; the typical healer may be a farmer, a barber, a shopkeeper, a blacksmith or even a wandering monk. The medical service they undertake, though not free of charge, is performed on ethical grounds and is non-commercial in nature. This low sustenance cost is one of the reasons why the tradition is so large, and widespread.

Natural Resource Base. Around 8,000 plant species and more than 200 animal and mineral sources are used in treating health problems in India's 4,639 ethnic communities [AICRPE, 1996]. This accounts for almost 50 per cent of the known flowering plants of India. There are huge numbers of written documents on the usage of these resources in the codified systems of medicines. It is interesting to observe that Indian knowledge about plants and plant products is not based on the application of western categories and approaches, such as chemistry and pharmacology. It is based on an indigenous system called *Dravya Guna Shastra,* the science of biological properties of natural materials. Establishing a bridge between Western biomedical science and Dravya Ghuna Shastra is complex, though functional links have been identified. Unfortunately, there is a lack of rigorous cross-cultural studies and, in fact, a well-accepted methodology for such studies is still missing.

The in-depth study to be done on a plant before it can be admitted into the indigenous Ayurvedic Materia Medica is quite impressive. It includes aspects like nomenclature, parts used, methods of purification, contraindications, effect on physiological systems, effect on body tissues, effect on organs, effect on the excretory system, qualities, metabolic activity, post-digestive effect, drug therapeutic class and processing strategies. This has resulted in around 25,000 plant drug formulations in the codified Ayurvedic system, while it is suggested that over 50,000 herbal drug formulations have been developed by India's ethnic communities.

Social and Cultural Aspects. The traditional Indian medical worldview recognizes the existence of body, mind, spirit and soul, and the therapies and practices cover these four dimensions. The concept of *swasthya*, or perfect health is, therefore, a combination of bio-physiological principles, metabolic processes, body channels, excretory processes, mental faculties, senses and the self. It is also understood that the external and the internal world of a being share the same principles, and that health requires a balance of the two.

Healing Hands of Shimoga

Generations of traditional knowledge and folk healing have been serving thousands of people faced with life threatening diseases all over the world. Near Shimoga, southern India, Mr Narayana Murthy is a living example of this. For the past eighteen years he is serving the people on Thursdays and Sundays of every week. These days are considered as *Siddhi varas*—days which gives good effect. The healer and his family are strong believers of God and do the daily rituals as per community rules. The blessing of the community deity (*Lakshmi Narasimha*) is an important factor which influences the patient's well-being and efficacy of the medicine given.

Healer Murthy treats the patients without any charge. The family's source of income is agriculture. Patients are allowed to put money in the metal box with small opening, without any condition and this amount is later used to meet the expenses of their community temple. Most cases that come to him are diagnosed cancer of different kinds (70% according to him) and people often consider this place as a final place of hope. Some patients carry laboratory reports of clinical diagnosis and hospital discharge summaries. His one day medication for the urinary calculi and medicines for heart blocks are a well-known remedy in Karnataka and adjacent states. According to the patients, their belief in the good heart and genuine mind of the healer is essential in the healing. As they state: *"We only want the medicine from his hands"*. Students and scientists of the Government Ayurvedic Medical College in Bangalore are learning and recording Murthy's cases, treatment and effects.

The Murthy family has established 30 acres of land with naturally grown medicinal plants and tree species. Healer Murthy views the plant as a living and a life-giving organism and a specific ritual is needed when collecting the required plant part. This ritual is a *pradhakshina*, encircling the divine body of the tree. He prays for the effect of the medicine and asks permission of the tree to take its part with medicinal properties. He says that this ritual bestows the effect of medicine. The ritual is also a sincere prayer for the benefit of each patient who comes to him for treatment.

Traditional medical knowledge is also diverse and specific to each eco-system and ethnic community, because of the special characteristics of resources, health needs and belief systems. There are certain common features, however, such as a very strict code of conduct followed by most barefoot doctors. They extend health care irrespective of a patient's personal work, caste, money and time. Certain prayers and offerings usually follow the collection of the medicinal plants and administration. Patients believe that certain healers have special healing powers, which is known as 'the power of the hand' or *Kaippunyam*.

The spiritual dimension of local health traditions is also included in communal meetings with folk healers and households. For example, some human disease conditions, particularly chronic skin ailments, are believed to have both material and spiritual causes, and the healer usually advises the patient to make a particular offering to the Snake God before starting the herbal treatment. In case of diseases caused by 'wind disorders in the body' the healers recite a special *mantra*, a kind of prayer, before starting the treatment with roots of four different plants. Traditional Indian literature also emphasises the spiritual dimension of the use of plants. It is obvious that including the spiritual dimension is essential to understanding the complexities and the potentialities of local health traditions in rural India.

The healers pass on their knowledge to younger successors who are selected on ethical criteria, which include qualities such as patience, strong faith in God, courage and a love of mankind. Some sociologists see this ethical screening as being 'too secretive'. But how could this explain the fact that at the start of the twenty-first century India continues to have around a million carriers of the oral health traditions spread throughout the country?

Erosion of Local Health Practices. Yet, there is a large-scale erosion of local health traditions. The average age of the traditional health worker is now over 50, and successors are limited in numbers. Even at household level, there are fewer households working with home remedies today. This deterioration of local health traditions has a major negative impact on the access to local health care, which is very important for a country like India. Despite erosion being quite evident, the reasons behind it are not clear. It is too simple to state that local health traditions are eroding because they are ineffective and unable to meet present needs. Plants have not lost their healing properties and the knowledge of plants in the traditions is still profound. At the same time there is a rapid resurgence of interest in natural medicine throughout the world. Pharmaceutical researchers acknowledge that screening plants on the basis of information derived from traditional knowledge saves billions of dollars in time and resources. The question, therefore, remains as to why health traditions are eroding despite their apparent potential.

The reasons for this erosion are political, economic and social rather than medical. Wild plants, wild animals and other natural resources used by traditional medicine are threatened due to degradation of natural habitats and, in specific cases, due to over-harvesting for commercial purposes. Urgent measures for conserving these genetic resources are necessary.

Influence of Modernization

Even though traditional medical knowledge serves a vast majority of the Indian population, government support for these traditions is very meagre. Only around 4 per cent of the annual health budget is allocated to the codified Indian systems of medicines, while the existence of local healers and local knowledge is not recognized in the Indian national health policy. Up to now there has been hardly any effort to recognize and codify the local health traditions in India.

Bio-prospecting. On the other hand, the interests of the pharmaceutical industry in herbal drugs [Wilgenburg, 1998], as well as the market for natural products, is growing. Laboratories are increasingly involved in isolating the active compounds of plants with medicinal properties for developing new drugs. Most of this research ends in patents. A few important examples of such commercialization from India are plants like *Phyllanthus niruri* for viral hepatitis, *Evolvulus alsinoides* and *Bacopa monnieri* for anxiety, *Gymnema sylvestre* for diabetes, *Garcinia indica* for obesity, and *Taxus wallichiana* for various types of cancer. It has been estimated that 74 per cent of the commercially used plant-based drugs have been developed on leads taken from indigenous knowledge. Needless to say that in most cases the local healers, who are the carriers of this knowledge, have no say in this commercialization. The source of this knowledge is seldom acknowledged and there is hardly any effort to share the benefits coming out of this commercialisation [Sinha *et al.*, 1998].

Public Health Care System. The present public health care system in India is dominated by western, technology-centred medicine, which depends heavily on external resources. It is estimated that only one-third of the population is covered by this system. In rural areas the coverage is much lower, sometimes as low as 3 per cent. In order to open up the rural markets for their products, companies with a western bias are actively trying to replace traditional beliefs and practices, presenting them as obsolete and irrational.

As a result of these and other developments, a section of the rural people in all social classes, including the poor, are giving up traditional health practices and turning to western medicine. But this medical system is increasingly unaffordable for common people. Moreover, in a few years time, and due to the new international trade and patents regime supervised by the World Trade Organization, modern pharmaceutical products are expected to become much more expensive than at present. Socio-economic surveys indicate that the single and largest cause of rural indebtedness in India is on account of health expenditure. This expense can be brought down considerably by promoting effective local health practices. ***(source: http://www.compasent.org/blog/wp.content/uploads)***

Annexure - III

Declaration of Alma-Ata

International Conference on Primary Health Care,
Alma-Ata, USSR, 6-12 September, 1978

The International Conference on Primary Health Care, meeting in Alma-Ata this twelfth day of September in the year nineteen hundred and seventy-eight, expressing the need for urgent action by all governments, all health and development workers, and the world community to protect and promote the health of all the people of the world, hereby makes the following:

Declaration

I

The Conference strongly reaffirms that health, which is a state of complete physical, mental and social well-being, and not merely the absence of disease or infirmity, is a fundamental human right and that the attainment of the highest possible level of health is a most important world-wide social goal whose realization requires the action of many other social and economic sectors in addition to the health sector.

II

The existing gross inequality in the health status of the people particularly between developed and developing countries as well as within countries is politically, socially and economically unacceptable and is, therefore, of common concern to all countries.

III

Economic and social development, based on a New International Economic Order, is of basic importance to the fullest attainment of health for all and to the reduction of the gap between the health status of the developing and developed countries. The promotion and protection of the health of the people is essential to sustained economic and social development and contributes to a better quality of life and to world peace.

IV

The people have the right and duty to participate individually and collectively in the planning and implementation of their healthcare.

V

Governments have a responsibility for the health of their people which can be fulfilled only by the provision of adequate health and social measures. A main social target of governments, international organizations and the whole world community in the coming decades should be the attainment by all peoples of the world by the year 2000 of a level of health that will permit them to lead a socially and economically productive life. Primary healthcare is the key to attaining this target as part of development in the spirit of social justice.

VI

Primary healthcare is essential healthcare based on practical, scientifically sound and socially acceptable methods and technology made universally accessible to individuals and families in the community through their full participation and at a cost that the community and country can afford to maintain at every stage of their development in the spirit of self-reliance and self-determination. It forms an integral part both of the country's health system, of which it is the central function and main focus, and of the overall social and economic development of the community. It is the first level of contact of individuals, the family and community with the national health system bringing healthcare as close as possible to where people live and work, and constitutes the first element of a continuing healthcare process.

VII

Primary Healthcare

1. Reflects and evolves from the economic conditions and socio-cultural and political characteristics of the country and its communities and is based on the application of the relevant results of social, biomedical and health services research and public health experience;
2. Addresses the main health problems in the community, providing promotive, preventive, curative and rehabilitative services accordingly;
3. Includes at least: education concerning prevailing health problems and the methods of preventing and controlling them; promotion of food supply and proper nutrition; an adequate supply of safe water and basic sanitation; maternal and child healthcare, including family planning; immunization against the major infectious diseases; prevention and control of locally endemic diseases; appropriate treatment of common diseases and injuries; and provision of essential drugs;
4. Involves, in addition to the health sector, all related sectors and aspects of national and community development, in particular agriculture, animal husbandry, food, industry, education, housing, public works, communications and other sectors; and demands the coordinated efforts of all those sectors;
5. Requires and promotes maximum community and individual self-reliance and participation in the planning, organization, operation and control of primary health care, making fullest use of local, national and other available

resources; and to this end develops through appropriate education the ability of communities to participate;
6. Should be sustained by integrated, functional and mutually supportive referral systems, leading to the progressive improvement of comprehensive healthcare for all, and giving priority to those most in need;
7. Relies, at local and referral levels, on health workers, including physicians, nurses, midwives, auxiliaries and community workers as applicable, as well as traditional practitioners as needed, suitably trained socially and technically to work as a health team and to respond to the expressed health needs of the community.

VIII

All governments should formulate national policies, strategies and plans of action to launch and sustain primary healthcare as part of a comprehensive national health system and in coordination with other sectors. To this end, it will be necessary to exercise political will, to mobilize the country's resources and to use available external resources rationally.

IX

All countries should cooperate in a spirit of partnership and service to ensure primary health care for all people since the attainment of health by people in anyone country directly concerns and benefits every other country. In this context the joint WHO-UNICEF report on primary health care constitutes a solid basis for the further development and operation of primary healthcare throughout the world.

X

An acceptable level of health for all the people of the world by the year 2000 can be attained through a fuller and better use of the world's resources, a considerable part of which is now spent on armaments and military conflicts. A genuine policy of independence, peace, detente and disarmament could and should release additional resources that could well be devoted to peaceful aims and in particular to the acceleration of social and economic development of which primary healthcare, as an essential part, should be allotted its proper share.

The International Conference on Primary Healthcare calls for urgent and effective national and international action to develop and implement primary healthcare throughout the world and particularly in developing countries in a spirit of technical cooperation and in keeping with a New International Economic Order. It urges governments, WHO and UNICEF, and other international organizations, as well as multilateral and bilateral agencies, non-governmental organizations, funding agencies, all health workers and the whole world community to support national and international commitment to primary health care and to channel increased technical and financial support to it, particularly in developing countries.

The Conference calls on all the aforementioned to collaborate in introducing, developing and maintaining primary healthcare in accordance with the spirit and content of this Declaration.

Source: www.who.int/publications/almaatadeclaration_en.pdf

Annexure - IV

Vaishali: An Experiment with Direct Democracy

Mahendra Prasad Singh

One of the earliest historical instances of republican democracy may be traced back to Vaishali, which was the name of both an ancient city and a state in modern north Bihar between the Ganga and the Nepal Himalayas. Piecing together literary, historical, and archeaological sources, Vaishali, at least the core city, is now identified with the Basarh village in the Vaishali district of present day Bihar. It was one of the 16 *mahajanapadas* (proto-states according to Historian R.S. Sharma) mentioned in a Buddhist text dated back to the sixth century BC. It was a confederation of numerous Vriji or Licchhavi tribes that governed themselves by anointed representative tribal chiefs forming a deliberative assembly that decided by majority vote. The anointed representatives were administered a rite of solemnization with the water of the Abhishak Pushkarni (Coronation Tank). Mahavir , the Jain Tirthankara, was born in the Jnatrika tribe there, and Buddha, who was born in the Shakya tribe in the republic of Kapilvastu and mostly resided in the monarchy of Magadha, also visited Vaishali a number of times. So did his favourite disciple Ananda who had a big stupa built after his name in Vaishali.

The second Buddhist Council was convened in Vaishali, following the first such Council held in Rajgriha in Magadha. The third Council was held in Pataliputra (Patna) and the fourth one in Pushpapur (Peshawar).

Ambapali (Amrapali), celebrated courtesan, also called 'Vaishali ki Nagarbadhu', was a cause of rivalries among the rulers of Vaishali and Magadha. She once invited Buddha and his disciples to her Amravana (mango garden) for a meal, and is said to have subsequently joined the Buddhist Order.

Historian Romila Thapar writes that the contemporary republican state's procedure of deliberation and decision-making by putting a matter to vote so impressed Buddha that he adopted it in the Buddhist Sangham.[2]

The political formations of the time, as is evident from the foregoing, were broadly divisible into republics and monarchies. The former were the predominant form in the Himalayan foothills ranging from the northwest to the middle Himalayas, and the latter mostly prevailed in the Ganga valley. The republican assembly was the governing body presided over by one of the representatives given the title of Raja. This was not a hereditary position. The Raja was aided by officials such as treasurer, commander of the armed forces, and a hierarchy of judicial officers. The Raja and other representatives in the ruling assembly were generally Kshatriyas. The Brahmanical sources were, by and large, inclined towards monarchy, whereas Buddhist sources, which rank Brahmans next to Kshatriyas, had a pronounced penchant for republican oligarchy.

According to Romila Thapar, the republican and monarchical systems 'were not mutually exclusive and a change from one to the other was not unheard of'. For example, Kambojin the north-west was transformed from a monarchy to a republic, and Vaishali moved in the opposite direction. It was conquered by Magadha . Thapar observes: 'The decline of tribal culture, in combination with a growing dependence on an agrarian economy, stimulated the growth of monarchies'.

Vaishali became a symbol of democracy and freedom during the anti-colonial struggle for independence against the British rule in India and it is still an insignia of Indian pride. A vast residential area of the middle class in Delhi is named Vaishali. The ancient site of Vaishali, maintained by the Archaeological Survey of India, is an important tourist spot

REFERENCES

Acharya Chatursen. *Vaishali ki Nagarvadhu*, Nai Dilli: Rajpal & Sons, 2010.

Sharma, R.S. *Ancient India*, New Delhi: National Council of Educational Research and Training, 1980.

Thapar, Romila. *A History of India*, Vol. I, London: Penguin Books, 1966.

Annexure - V

National Rural Health Mission (NRHM): A Survey Report

(To What Extent are the Panchayats participating in the Health Policy?)

Bidyut Mohanty

Introduction

Just like the scheme on the Mahatma Gandhi National Rural Employment Guarantee Act (MGNREGS), the National Rural Health Mission (NRHM) is yet another right-based and flagship scheme which was introduced in 2005 till 2012 in eighteen states to improve the health delivery system in the rural areas. It was introduced by the Ministry of Health and Welfare, Government of India. The states in which it has been introduced are: Arunachal Pradesh, Assam, Bihar, Chhatttisgarh, Himachal Pradesh, Jharkhand, Jammu & Kashmir, Manipur, Meghalaya, Mizoram, Madhya Pradesh, Nagaland, Odisha, Rajasthan, Sikkim, Tripura, Uttarakhand and Uttar Pradesh. In the rest of the country, the backward districts came under the scheme. Recently the scheme has been renamed as National Health Mission (NHM), under which the towns and cities will be covered.

Objectives of NRHM

Under this scheme the term health has been defined in a more comprehensive manner. It is defined not only in terms of well-being of mental and physical health but also improving sanitation, safe drinking water, shelter and assured livelihood. The ultimate goal is to have healthy human resources to meet Millennium Development Goals (MDGs) which are coming to an end in 2015. Further, under this scheme, equal emphasis has been given on all aspects of health such as promotive, curative, preventive and rehabilitative. The branches of treatment consist of allopathic, and Ayush. Keeping this in mind, about one million health personnel out of which 0.8 million are Accredited Social Health Activists (ASHA) are recruited locally and are trained to act as health educators and facilitators at the community level.

The introduction of the scheme became absolutely necessary since our health indicators are not that satisfactory. First of all our maternal mortality rate (254 per hundred thousand population), infant mortality rate (47 per thousand live births) and incidence of malnutrition among the children (46% of the total child population) are worse than the world average. Yet the share of GDP spent on the health sector was abysmally low that is only 1.0 per cent. Even though the Prime Minister declared the Twelfth Five Year Plan as the plan for health, the share of GDP increased to 1.58 which is very small. Even the former President Pratibha Patil had suggested in Parliament that the share should be raised to 2.5 per cent. Besides, the High Level Expert Group (HLEG) and Steering Committee set up by the Planning Commission had suggested raising the spending on health by 2.5 per cent of GDP keeping the inadequate infrastructures and human resources in mind.

The Central Role of Panchayats

Yet another feature of the scheme is that it highlighted a bottom-up approach through a participatory planning by the community and panchayats. Additionally, the formation of the Health, Nutrition and Sanitation Committee at the panchayat level has been yet another novel approach to address health issues. It is so because the Committee comprises panchayat members, micro credit members, community workers,etc. The Committee is entitled to Rs.'10,000 as an untied fund per year to spend wherever it deems necessary. The grant can be enhanced if the Committee can show the proper utilization certificate of funds.

In order to give a sense of ownership it is proposed to set up a platform to involve Panchayati Raj Institutions (PRIs) and community to manage the primary health programme and infrastructure. In order to do that it was necessary to train and enhance the capacity of the elected representatives. The aim was that the panchayat members would be able to own, control and manage public health services. In other words, the panchayats have an important role to play in so far as the health issues of the area is concerned.

The year 2012 is the end year of the Mission. It is important to know as to what extent the elected representatives in general and women representatives (EWRs) in particular know about the flagship programme such as NRHM. In order to find out the ground realities, the Institute of Social Sciences, New Delhi conducted a survey by fielding a structured questionnaire among 400 elected women representatives representing 20 states. Those states are: Arunachal Pradesh, Assam, Andhra (though the panchayats are non-functional), Bihar, Chhattisgarh, Goa, Gujarat, Haryana, Himachal Pradesh, Jammu & Kashmir, Karnataka, Madhya Pradesh, Maharashtra, Manipur, Odisha, Rajasthan, Sikkim, Uttar Pradesh, Uttarakhand and West Bengal.

The Findings

The overall conclusions which emerged by interviewing 400 elected women representatives who are predominantly from gram panchayats are:

Panchayats play a minimal role in so far as the implementation of NRHM is concerned. Not a single woman who was interviewed by us talked about the preparation of a health plan which has been mandatory under the NRHM.

Secondly, the objectives of NRHM in terms of promoting good health, rehabilitating the patients in post care situations and preventing occurrences of epidemics have been fulfilled.

However, in terms of reaching out to pregnant women in order to increase institutional delivery as well as to reduce maternal and infant mortality, the NRHM's is strategy has been successful. Of course, the success may partly be due to an earlier scheme called *Janani Surakshya Yojana.*

The Socio-Economic Background of the EWRs

Of the total respondents 75 per cent were from village panchayats level and were predominantly ward members. Block panchayat members constituted 8 per cent and that of zilla panchayats was 9 per cent and the rest comprised civil society members. With regard to age composition of the EWRs , it is important to note that 55 per cent of the EWRs were in the age group of 25-49 and 9 per cent were in the age group of below 20 years. In other words, 64 per cent were in the age group reproductive phase for whom NRHM is quite important. The age group which had crossed the reproductive span was 26 per cent. The respondents in the age group of above 60 constituted only 2 per cent.

It is important to note that out of the total respondents SC constituted 29 per cent; ST 21 per cent; OBC 17 per cent; and general 26 per cent. In terms of the occupation, 41 per cent of the women replied that they were householders followed by agriculture 27 per cent; and labour 14 per cent. It is interesting to note that 7 per cent of them said that they were in service. We also enquired about the duration of their leadership. Eighty-two per cent of them replied that they were first timers. Second timers constituted a poor 13 per cent. With regard to their educational qualifications it is important to note that almost 80 per cent of them were educated of which 11 per cent had college degrees, 17 per cent had education up to the Higher Secondary, 29 per cent were from middle school level and primary level of education.

Nature of Healthcare Services available in the Panchayats

At the level of gram panchayat the existence of Primary Health Centre/Community Health Centre are absolutely necessary. Fifty-seven per cent of the EWRs reported that they have PHC but a whopping 41 per cent of them said 'no'. Out of 57 per cent women who responded positively, 54 per cent said that the PHC/CSC has its own building. But it is encouraging to note that 90 per cent of the structures were made up of *pucca* houses.

In responding to the query as to whether doctors visit the health centre, 51 per cent of them replied that 'yes they do' but 40 per cent were negative. Nine per cent said that they do not know. How often do the doctors visit the centre? To this 45 per cent out of 51 per cent said daily, 25 per cent weekly and 29 per cent said monthly. In so far as the availability of the para-medical personnel in the centre is concerned 53 per cent of them said 'yes' but 36 per cent of them replied in the negative.

Availability of Medicine

One of the important components of NRHM is to avail of basic medicines distributed free to the villagers. Fifty-five per cent of the total EWRs interviewed pointed out that they do get medicines but 45 per cent said that they were not available. Do they get medicines free? To this out of 55 per cent, 88 per cent said yes they do. But the remaining 12 per cent of the women said that they have to pay for the medicines.

Knowledge about ASHA

One of the important strategies of the NRHM is to reach out to the pregnant women through the Accredited Social Health Activist to improve the health of the women as well as to encourage them to use institutional delivery. The objective is to reduce both maternal and infant mortality. ASHA acts as the community worker, as a bridge between the health personnel and village women. Since the majority of the interviewees were in the age group of the reproductive span it is important to know as to what percentage of them at least know about the ASHA *karmee*. It is indeed heartening to know that 89 per cent said that they were aware of the activities of ASHA. It is also interesting to know wherever ASHA has not appointed Anganwadi workers to do the necessary job. In other places like Himachal Pradesh both ASHA and Anganwadi workers went together to reach out to the pregnant women. The women talked about the activities of ASHA. Almost all of them observed that she encouraged pregnant women to get registered at the nearest CSC. Women from the south said that ASHA also talked about the family planning and measures to prevent the onslaught of HIV. Some replied that ASHA was involved in vaccination, and had a health kit with her. However, 12 per cent of the EWRs maintained that they are unaware of the activities of ASHA. It is heartening to know that almost all the EWRs knew that both the ASHA and the pregnant women were paid provided women delivered in the hospital. Everybody also knew that there were provisions of transport to take the pregnant woman when she was in labour though it was named differently in different states. For example, in Odisha it is known as Janani Express but in Bihar it is known differently. However, it is important to know that transport is hardly available when it is needed. It is also well known that both ASHA and the pregnant woman get some remuneration after the woman delivers the baby. However, most of the times the pregnant woman has to pay much more than whatever she gets from the government. The last but not the least point to note that one important component of NRHM, namely, AYUSH has been completely sidelined since nobody talked about it.

Do the Panchayat Members Know How She is Appointed?

Sixty-five per cent of them said that the panchayat had the primary duty to appoint the ASHA. But the rest pointed out that the BDO, Tehsildar, etc., could be the appointing agency.

We got a very interesting reply to our query as to the knowledge regarding NRHM and its objectives. Only 50 per cent were aware of NRHM. But another 50 per cent had no knowledge about the grand objectives of NRHM! It could be due partly to renaming the health scheme in the state using an appropriate name. As for example, the Odisha government has titled it as MAMATA Health Scheme or Mitanin programme (Chhattisgarh). But most of these programmes are geared towards reaching out to pregnant women only. The preventive aspect of the scheme hardly gets reflected. To the question namely, 'do panchayats get any NRHM-related funding?' 33 per cent said 'yes', whereas 56 per cent said no and 11 per cent did not know. The amount received under the heading of NRHM, varied from ₹ 50,000 to ₹ 10,00,000. Fifty-three per cent vouched for the first amount and the last one was supported by 4 per cent. However, 36 per cent replied saying that they were ignorant about the grant.

Knowledge about the Standing Committee on Health

Yet another query was on the knowledge about the Standing Committee on Health, Nutrition and Sanitation. It is important because it is the monitoring agency of the implementation of the scheme. It is important to know that 55 per cent of the total EWRs surveyed, were aware of the committee. But 45 per cent did not know anything about it. About the periodicity of the meeting of the committee members 76 per cent out of 55 per cent said that the committee met monthly but 9 per cent said it met weekly. With regard to the range of activities, 35 per cent said that they were not aware of any activities of the committee but 24 per cent said that the committee looked after the vaccination and other health-related work. Sixteen per cent replied that it monitored sanitation related matter. Fourteen per cent of them said that the committee looked after development issues such as construction of roads. Finally we were curious to know if siphoning of health related funds takes place or not. Unfortunately, many ward members felt constrained in the presence of the pradhans or other officials. So 55 per cent of them replied that no leakage had been taking place out of funds meant for healthcare. Twenty-six per cent of them said that they were not aware of such a leakage and only 19 per cent said it ran into lakhs. According to them, the Anganwadi worker, sarpanch and BDO were responsible for such a leakage.

Source: Based on a survey conducted by the ISS, New Delhi among four hundred elected women representatives.

List of Contributors

Almas Ali, Senior Fellow, ISS, New Delhi.

Anne Stenhammer, is Regional Programme Director, UN Women, New Delhi.

Aslak Brun, Aslak Brun is Deputy Chief of Mission, Royal Norwegian Embassy, New Delhi.

Bidyut Mohanty, Head, Women's Studies Unit, Institute of Social Sciences.

Fredrika Meijer, is the Country Representative, UNFPA, New Delhi.

George Mathew Chairman, Institute of Social Sciences, New Delhi.

K.B. Saxena Visiting Professor Council for Social Development, New Delhi.

Madhulika Banerjee Associate Professor, Department of Political Science, Delhi University, Delhi.

Mahendra Prasad Singh, is retired Professor in the Department of Political Science, Delhi University.

Natasha Das, Medical Communicator, New Delhi.

Nupur Tiwari, is Assistant Professor Rural Development and Panchayati Raj, Indian Institute of Public Administration, New Delhi.

Ritu Priya, is Professor, Centre for Social Medicine and Community Health, Jawaharlal Nehru University, New Delhi.

Saurabh Gahlote, is Medical Superintendent, Vinayak Hospital, NOIDA.

Suraj Kumar, Head, Governance Program, UN Women, New Delhi.

V. Kishore Chandra, Deo is Honourable Union Minister for Panchayati Raj and Tribal Affairs.

Vandana Prasad, National Convenor of Public Health Resource Network, New Delhi.

Varsha Das, Ex-Director, National Gandhi Museum, New Delhi.

Index